CONNECTED MAT

Stretching -and- Shrinking

Understanding Similarity

Glenda Lappan, Elizabeth Difanis Phillips,
James T. Fey, Susan N. Friel

PEARSON

Boston, Massachusetts • Chandler, Arizona • Glenview, Illinois • Hoboken, New Jersey

Connected Mathematics® was developed at Michigan State University with financial support from the Michigan State University Office of the Provost, Computing and Technology, and the College of Natural Science.

 This material is based upon work supported by the National Science Foundation under Grant No. MDR 9150217 and Grant No. ESI 9986372. Opinions expressed are those of the authors and not necessarily those of the Foundation.

As with prior editions of this work, the authors and administration of Michigan State University preserve a tradition of devoting royalties from this publication to support activities sponsored by the MSU Mathematics Education Enrichment Fund.

13-digit ISBN 978-0-13-327448-6
10-digit ISBN 0-13-327448-9
8 9 10 V011 17 16 15

PEARSON

A Team of Experts

Glenda Lappan is a University Distinguished Professor in the Program in Mathematics Education (PRIME) and the Department of Mathematics at Michigan State University. Her research and development interests are in the connected areas of students' learning of mathematics and mathematics teachers' professional growth and change related to the development and enactment of K–12 curriculum materials.

Elizabeth Difanis Phillips is a Senior Academic Specialist in the Program in Mathematics Education (PRIME) and the Department of Mathematics at Michigan State University. She is interested in teaching and learning mathematics for both teachers and students. These interests have led to curriculum and professional development projects at the middle school and high school levels, as well as projects related to the teaching and learning of algebra across the grades.

James T. Fey is a Professor Emeritus at the University of Maryland. His consistent professional interest has been development and research focused on curriculum materials that engage middle and high school students in problem-based collaborative investigations of mathematical ideas and their applications.

Susan N. Friel is a Professor of Mathematics Education in the School of Education at the University of North Carolina at Chapel Hill. Her research interests focus on statistics education for middle-grade students and, more broadly, on teachers' professional development and growth in teaching mathematics K–8.

With... Yvonne Grant and Jacqueline Stewart

Yvonne Grant teaches mathematics at Portland Middle School in Portland, Michigan. Jacqueline Stewart is a recently retired high school teacher of mathematics at Okemos High School in Okemos, Michigan. Both Yvonne and Jacqueline have worked on a variety of activities related to the development, implementation, and professional development of the CMP curriculum since its beginning in 1991.

Development Team

CMP3 Authors

Glenda Lappan, University Distinguished Professor, Michigan State University

Elizabeth Difanis Phillips, Senior Academic Specialist, Michigan State University

James T. Fey, Professor Emeritus, University of Maryland

Susan N. Friel, Professor, University of North Carolina – Chapel Hill

With...

Yvonne Grant, Portland Middle School, Michigan

Jacqueline Stewart, Mathematics Consultant, Mason, Michigan

In Memory of... William M. Fitzgerald, Professor (Deceased), Michigan State University, who made substantial contributions to conceptualizing and creating CMP1.

Administrative Assistant

Michigan State University
Judith Martus Miller

Support Staff

Michigan State University
Undergraduate Assistants:
Bradley Robert Corlett, Carly Fleming,
Erin Lucian, Scooter Nowak

Development Assistants

Michigan State University
Graduate Research Assistants:
Richard "Abe" Edwards, Nic Gilbertson,
Funda Gonulates, Aladar Horvath,
Eun Mi Kim, Kevin Lawrence, Jennifer
Nimtz, Joanne Philhower, Sasha Wang

Assessment Team

Maine
Falmouth Public Schools
Falmouth Middle School: Shawn Towle

Michigan
Ann Arbor Public Schools
Tappan Middle School
Anne Marie Nicoll-Turner

Portland Public Schools
Portland Middle School
Holly DeRosia, Yvonne Grant

Traverse City Area Public Schools
Traverse City East Middle School
Jane Porath, Mary Beth Schmitt

Traverse City West Middle School
Jennifer Rundio, Karrie Tufts

Ohio
Clark-Shawnee Local Schools
Rockway Middle School: Jim Mamer

Content Consultants

Michigan State University
Peter Lappan, Professor Emeritus,
Department of Mathematics

Normandale Community College
Christopher Danielson, Instructor,
Department of Mathematics & Statistics

University of North Carolina – Wilmington
Dargan Frierson, Jr., Professor, Department
of Mathematics & Statistics

Student Activities
Michigan State University
Brin Keller, Associate Professor,
Department of Mathematics

Consultants

Indiana
Purdue University
Mary Bouck, Mathematics Consultant

Michigan
Oakland Schools
Valerie Mills, Mathematics Education
Supervisor
Mathematics Education Consultants:
Geraldine Devine, Dana Gosen

Ellen Bacon, Independent Mathematics
Consultant

New York
University of Rochester
Jeffrey Choppin, Associate Professor

Ohio
University of Toledo
Debra Johanning, Associate Professor

Pennsylvania
University of Pittsburgh
Margaret Smith, Professor

Texas
University of Texas at Austin
Emma Trevino, Supervisor of
Mathematics Programs, The Dana Center

Mathematics for All Consulting
Carmen Whitman, Mathematics Consultant

....

Reviewers

Michigan
Ionia Public Schools
Kathy Dole, Director of Curriculum
and Instruction

Grand Valley State University
Lisa Kasmer, Assistant Professor

Portland Public Schools
Teri Keusch, Classroom Teacher

Minnesota
Hopkins School District 270
Michele Luke, Mathematics Coordinator

....

Field Test Sites for CMP3

Michigan
Ann Arbor Public Schools
Tappan Middle School
Anne Marie Nicoll-Turner*

Portland Public Schools
Portland Middle School: Mark Braun,
Angela Buckland, Holly DeRosia,
Holly Feldpausch, Angela Foote,
Yvonne Grant*, Kristin Roberts,
Angie Stump, Tammi Wardwell

Traverse City Area Public Schools
Traverse City East Middle School
Ivanka Baic Berkshire, Brenda Dunscombe,
Tracie Herzberg, Deb Larimer, Jan Palkowski,
Rebecca Perreault, Jane Porath*,
Robert Sagan, Mary Beth Schmitt*

Traverse City West Middle School
Pamela Alfieri, Jennifer Rundio,
Maria Taplin, Karrie Tufts*

Maine
Falmouth Public Schools
Falmouth Middle School: Sally Bennett,
Chris Driscoll, Sara Jones, Shawn Towle*

Minnesota
Minneapolis Public Schools
Jefferson Community School
Leif Carlson*,
Katrina Hayek Munsisoumang*

Ohio
Clark-Shawnee Local Schools
Reid School: Joanne Gilley
Rockway Middle School: Jim Mamer*
Possum School: Tami Thomas

*Indicates a Field Test Site Coordinator

Stretching and Shrinking

Understanding Similarity

Looking Ahead

A map is a scale drawing of the place it represents. You can use a map to find actual distances to any place in the world. **How** can you estimate the distance from Cape Town, South Africa to Port Elizabeth, South Africa?

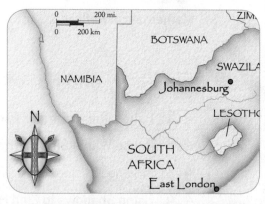

Suppose that you want to find the width of a river that is too wide to measure directly. **How** can you use similar triangles to find the distance across the river?

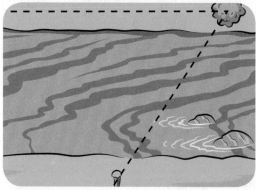

Here is a picture of Duke, a real dog. If you know the scale factor between Duke and the picture, **how** can you determine how long Duke is from his nose to the tip of his tail?

You probably use the word *similar* in everyday conversation. For example, you might say that one song sounds similar to another song. You may also say that your friend's bike is similar to yours.

In many cases, you might use the word *similar* to describe objects and images that are the same shape but not the same size.

A floor plan of a house has the same shape as the actual house, but it is much smaller. The images on a movie screen are the same shape as the real people and objects they depict, but they are much larger. You can order your school portrait in a variety of sizes, but your face will have the same shape in each photo.

In this Unit, you will learn what it means for two shapes to be mathematically similar. The ideas you learn can help you answer questions like those on the previous page.

Mathematical Highlights

Understanding Similarity

In *Stretching and Shrinking*, you will learn the mathematical meaning of similarity, explore the properties of similar figures, and use similarity to solve problems.

You will learn how to

- Identify similar figures by comparing corresponding sides and angles

- Use scale factors and ratios to describe relationships among the side lengths, perimeters, and areas of similar figures

- Construct similar figures (scale drawings) using informal methods, scale factors, and geometric tools

- Use algebraic rules to produce similar figures and recognize when a rule shrinks or enlarges a figure

- Predict the ways that stretching or shrinking a figure will affect side lengths, angle measures, perimeters, and areas

- Use the properties of similarity to find distances and heights that cannot be measured directly

- Use scale factors or ratios to find missing side lengths in a pair of similar figures

When you encounter a new problem, it is a good idea to ask yourself questions. In this Unit, you might ask questions such as:

What determines whether two shapes are similar?

What is the same and what is different about two similar figures?

When figures are similar, **how** are the side lengths, areas, and scale factors related?

How can I use similar figures to find missing measurements?

Mathematical Practices and Habits of Mind

In the *Connected Mathematics* curriculum you will develop an understanding of important mathematical ideas by solving problems and reflecting on the mathematics involved. Every day, you will use "habits of mind" to make sense of problems and apply what you learn to new situations. Some of these habits are described by the *Common Core State Standards for Mathematical Practices* (MP).

MP1 Make sense of problems and persevere in solving them.

When using mathematics to solve a problem, it helps to think carefully about

- data and other facts you are given and what additional information you need to solve the problem;
- strategies you have used to solve similar problems and whether you could solve a related simpler problem first;
- how you could express the problem with equations, diagrams, or graphs;
- whether your answer makes sense.

MP2 Reason abstractly and quantitatively.

When you are asked to solve a problem, it often helps to

- focus first on the key mathematical ideas;
- check that your answer makes sense in the problem setting;
- use what you know about the problem setting to guide your mathematical reasoning.

MP3 Construct viable arguments and critique the reasoning of others.

When you are asked to explain why a conjecture is correct, you can

- show some examples that fit the claim and explain why they fit;
- show how a new result follows logically from known facts and principles.

When you believe a mathematical claim is incorrect, you can

- show one or more counterexamples—cases that don't fit the claim;
- find steps in the argument that do not follow logically from prior claims.

MP4 Model with mathematics.

When you are asked to solve problems, it often helps to

- think carefully about the numbers or geometric shapes that are the most important factors in the problem, then ask yourself how those factors are related to each other;
- express data and relationships in the problem with tables, graphs, diagrams, or equations, and check your result to see if it makes sense.

MP5 Use appropriate tools strategically.

When working on mathematical questions, you should always

- decide which tools are most helpful for solving the problem and why;
- try a different tool when you get stuck.

MP6 Attend to precision.

In every mathematical exploration or problem-solving task, it is important to

- think carefully about the required accuracy of results; is a number estimate or geometric sketch good enough, or is a precise value or drawing needed?
- report your discoveries with clear and correct mathematical language that can be understood by those to whom you are speaking or writing.

MP7 Look for and make use of structure.

In mathematical explorations and problem solving, it is often helpful to

- look for patterns that show how data points, numbers, or geometric shapes are related to each other;
- use patterns to make predictions.

MP8 Look for and express regularity in repeated reasoning.

When results of a repeated calculation show a pattern, it helps to

- express that pattern as a general rule that can be used in similar cases;
- look for shortcuts that will make the calculation simpler in other cases.

You will use all of the Mathematical Practices in this Unit. Sometimes, when you look at a Problem, it is obvious which practice is most helpful. At other times, you will decide on a practice to use during class explorations and discussions. After completing each Problem, ask yourself:

- What mathematics have I learned by solving this Problem?
- What Mathematical Practices were helpful in learning this mathematics?

Enlarging and Reducing Shapes

In this Investigation, you will make **scale drawings** of figures. Your scale drawings will have the same shape as the original figure, but may be larger or smaller. The drawings will help you explore how some properties of a shape change when the shape is enlarged or reduced.

Common Core State Standards

7.RP.A.2 Recognize and represent proportional relationships between quantities.

7.G.A.1 Solve problems involving scale drawings of geometric figures, including computing actual lengths and areas from a scale drawing and reproducing a scale drawing at a different scale.

7.G.A.2 Draw (freehand, with ruler and protractor, and with technology) geometric shapes with given conditions. Focus on constructing triangles from three measures of angles or sides, noticing when the conditions determine a unique triangle, more than one triangle, or no triangle.

Also 7.RP.A.2b, 7.G.B.6

1.1 Solving a Mystery
An Introduction to Similarity

The Mystery Club at P.I. Middle School meets monthly. Members watch videos, discuss novels, play "whodunit" games, and talk about real-life mysteries. One day, a member announces that the school is having a contest. A teacher in disguise will appear for a few minutes at school each day for a week. Any student can pay $1 for a guess at the identity of the mystery teacher. The student with the first correct guess wins a prize.

The Mystery Club decides to enter the contest together. Each member brings a camera to school in hopes of getting a picture of the mystery teacher.

One of Daphne's photos looks like the picture below. Daphne has a copy of the *P.I. Monthly* magazine shown in the picture. The *P.I. Monthly* magazine is 10 inches high. She thinks she can use the magazine and the picture to estimate the teacher's height.

- What do you think Daphne has in mind? Use the picture and the information about the height of the magazine to estimate the teacher's height. Explain your reasoning.

- The teacher advisor to the Mystery Club says that the picture is similar to the actual scene. What do you suppose the adviser means by *similar*? Is it different from saying that two students in your class are similar?

Michelle, Daphne, and Mukesh are the officers of the Mystery Club. Mukesh designs this flier to attract new members.

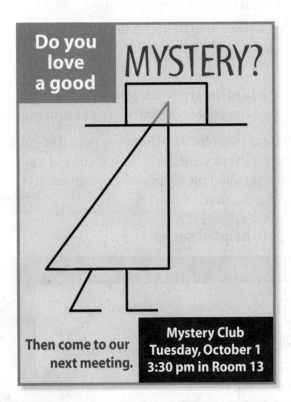

Daphne wants to make a large poster to publicize the next meeting. She wants to redraw the club's logo, "Super Sleuth," in a larger size. Michelle shows her a clever way to enlarge the figure by using rubber bands.

Instructions for Stretching a Figure

1. Make a "two-band stretcher" by tying the ends of two identical rubber bands together. (The rubber bands should be the same width and length.) Bands about 3 inches long work well.

2. Take the sheet with the figure you want to enlarge and tape it to your desk. Next to it, tape a blank sheet of paper. If you are right-handed, put the blank sheet on the right. If you are left-handed, put it on the left (see the diagram below).

3. With your finger, hold down one end of the rubber-band stretcher on point *P*. Point *P* is called the *anchor point*. It must stay in the same spot.

4. Put a pencil in the other end of the stretcher. Stretch the rubber bands with the pencil until the knot is on the outline of your picture.

5. Keep the rubber bands taut (stretched). Move your pencil to guide the knot around the picture. Your pencil will draw a copy of the picture. The new picture is called the **image** of the original. It is also a scale drawing of the original.

Left-handed setup

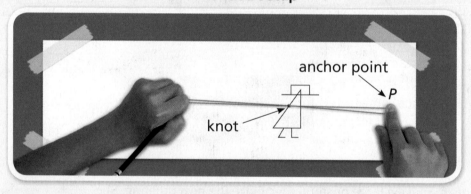

Right-handed setup

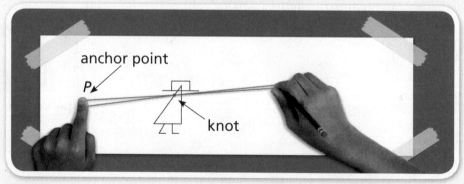

• How are the original shape and its image alike? Different?

Problem 1.1

Use the rubber-band method to enlarge the figure on the Mystery Club flier. Draw the figure as carefully as you can, so you can compare the size and shape of the image to the size and shape of the original figure.

A Describe how the original figure and the image are alike and how they are different. Compare these features:

- the general shapes of the two figures
- the lengths of the line segments in the hats and bodies
- the areas and perimeters of the hats and bodies
- the angles in the hats and bodies
- the distance of corresponding points on each figure from P

Explain each comparison you make. For example, you may find that two lengths are different. Be sure to tell which lengths you are comparing and explain how they are different.

B Use your rubber-band stretcher to enlarge another simple figure, such as a circle or a square.

   1. Compare the general shapes, lengths, areas, perimeters, and angles of the original figure and the image.

   2. Would your comparisons in part (1) change if the location of P were changed? Explain why or why not.

C The original figure and its image are *similar figures*. What do you think similar means in mathematical terms? What things are the same about these similar figures? What is different?

 **A C E** Homework starts on page 16.

1.2 Scaling Up and Down
Corresponding Sides and Angles

In the last Problem, you worked with images, or scale drawings, that were similar to the original. Those scale drawings were larger than the original figure. In this Problem, you will work with scale drawings that are smaller than the original. You will also learn more about what it means for figures to be *similar*.

When you study similar figures, you often compare their sides and angles. To compare the parts correctly, mathematicians use the terms **corresponding sides** and **corresponding angles.** In every pair of similar figures, each side of one figure has a corresponding side in the other figure. Also, each angle has a corresponding angle.

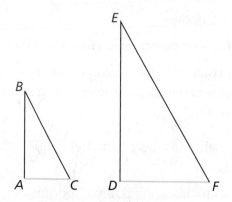

Corresponding angles
B and *E*
A and *D*
C and *F*

Corresponding sides
AC and *DF*
AB and *DE*
BC and *EF*

Recall that there are two ways to identify angles.

You can identify an angle with three letters. The angles in the small triangle on the previous page have the following names:

Angle BAC	or	$\angle BAC$
Angle BCA	or	$\angle BCA$
Angle ABC	or	$\angle ABC$

Notice that the letter identifying the vertex of an angle is always the middle letter in its name. For example, point A is the vertex of $\angle BAC$.

You can also name an angle by its vertex. It is important to use this method only when it is clear which angle you are referring to.

$\angle BAC$	can also be called	$\angle A$
$\angle BCA$	can also be called	$\angle C$
$\angle ABC$	can also be called	$\angle B$

- What names would you give the angles of the large triangle?

Did You Know?

Measurement is often used in police work. For example, some stores with cameras place a spot on the wall 6 feet from the floor. When a person standing near the wall is filmed, this makes it easier to estimate the person's height. Investigators take measurements of tire marks at the scene of auto accidents to help them estimate the speed of the vehicles involved. Photographs and molds of footprints help the police determine the shoe size, type of shoe, and weight of the person who made the prints.

Daphne thinks the rubber-band method is clever, but she believes the school copier can make more accurate copies in a greater variety of sizes. She makes a copy of "Super Sleuth" with the size factor set at 75%. Then, she makes a copy with a setting of 150%. The results are shown below.

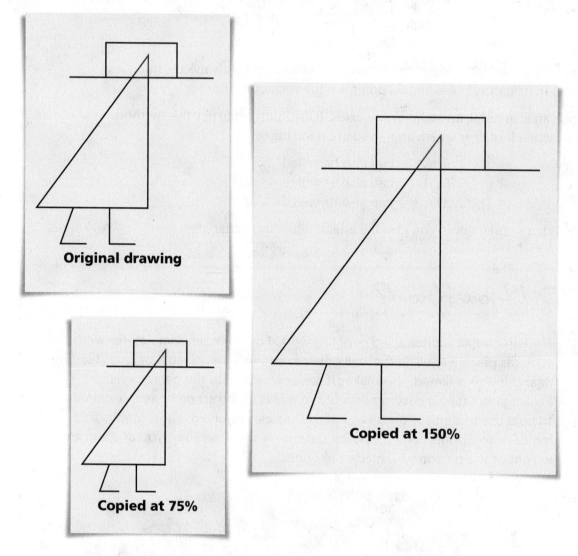

Original drawing

Copied at 75%

Copied at 150%

- How are these copies of the original logo like the copy you made with the rubber-band stretchers? How are these copies different from the rubber-band stretcher copy?

- How are these copies like the original? How are they different?

Problem 1.2

A Use the figures on the previous page. For each copy of Super Sleuth, do the following:

1. Describe how the side lengths compare to the corresponding side lengths in the original figure.

2. Describe how the angle measures compare to the corresponding angle measures in the original figure.

3. Describe how the perimeter of the triangle in each copy compares to the perimeter of the triangle in the original figure.

4. Describe how the area of the triangle in each copy compares to the area of the triangle in the original figure.

B How do the relationships in the size comparisons you made in Question A relate to the copier size factors used?

C 1. If two figures are similar, what is the same about the figures and what is different?

2. If you wanted to achieve a 150% increase with the rubber-band method, what would you do?

ACE Homework starts on page 16.

Applications

For Exercises 1 and 2, use the drawing at the right, which shows a person standing next to a ranger's outlook tower.

1. Find the approximate height of the tower if the person is

    a. 6 feet tall

    b. 5 feet 6 inches tall

2. Find the approximate height of the person if the tower is

    a. 28 feet tall

    b. 36 feet tall

3. Copy square *ABCD* and anchor point *P* onto a sheet of paper. Use the rubber-band method to enlarge the figure. Then, answer parts (a)–(e) below.

    a. How do the side lengths of the original figure compare to the side lengths of the image?

    b. How does the perimeter of the original figure compare to the perimeter of the image?

    c. How do the angle measures of the original figure compare to the angle measures of the image?

    d. How does the area of the original figure compare to the area of the image? How many copies of the original figure would it take to cover the image?

    e. How does the distance between each point in the original figure and *P* compare to the corresponding distances in the image?

4. Copy parallelogram *ABCD* and anchor point *P* onto a sheet of paper. Use the rubber-band method to enlarge the figure. Then, answer parts (a)–(e) from Exercise 3 for your diagram.

5. The diagram on the left is the floor plan for a model house. The diagram on the right is a scale drawing of the floor plan. The scale drawing was made by reducing the original on a copy machine.

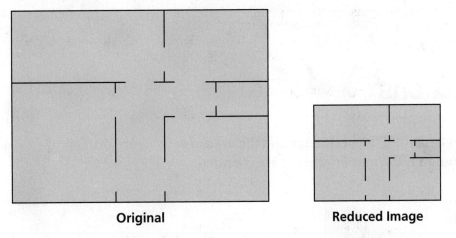

Original   Reduced Image

   a. Estimate the copier size factor used. Give your answer as a percent.

   b. How do the segment lengths in the original plan compare to the corresponding segment lengths in the reduced image?

   c. Compare the area of the entire original floor plan to the area of the entire reduced image. Then, do the same with one room in the plan. Is the relationship between the areas of the rooms the same as the relationship between the areas of the whole plans? Explain.

   d. The scale on the original plan is 1 inch = 1 foot. This means that 1 inch on the floor plan represents 1 foot on the model house. What is the scale on the reduced plan?

6. **Multiple Choice** Suppose you reduce the design below with a copy machine. Which of the following can be the image?

A.    B.   C.   D.

7. Suppose you copy a drawing of a polygon using the given size factor. How will the side lengths, angle measures, and perimeter of the image compare to those of the original?

   a. 200%   **b.** 150%   **c.** 50%   **d.** 75%

Connections

For Exercises 8–11, find the perimeter and the area of each figure. In Exercises 10 and 11, the measurements are rounded.

8.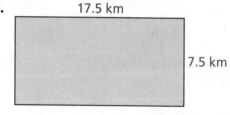

9.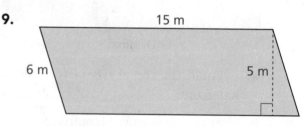

10.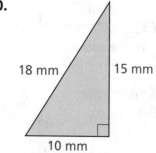

11.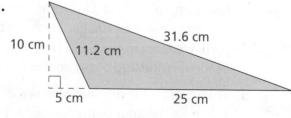

12. Copy hexagon *ABCDEF* and anchor point *P* onto a sheet of paper. Make an enlargement of the hexagon using your two-band stretcher.

  a. How do the side lengths of the two hexagons compare?

  b. How do the angles of the hexagons compare?

  c. How do the areas of the hexagons compare?

  d. How do the perimeters of the hexagons compare?

13. Find the given percent of each number. Show your work.

  a. 25% of 120   **b.** 80% of 120

  c. 120% of 80   **d.** 70% of 150

  e. 150% of 200   **f.** 200% of 150

14. Multiple Choice What is the 5% sales tax on a $14.00 compact disc?

  A. $0.07   **B.** $ 0.70

  C. $7.00   **D.** $70.00

15. Multiple Choice What is the 15% service tip on a $25.50 dinner in a restaurant?

  F. $1.70   **G.** $ 3.83

  H. $5.10   **J.** $38.25

16. **Multiple Choice** What is the 28% tax on a $600,000 cash prize?

    A. $16,800   **B.** $ 21,429

    C. $168,000   **D.** $214,290

17. **Multiple Choice** What is the 7.65% Social Security/Medicare tax on a paycheck of $430?

    F. $3.29   **G.** $5.62

    H. $32.90   **J.** $60.13

18. One angle measure is given for each of the parallelograms below.

   - Find the measure of the other three angles in the parallelogram.

   - List all pairs of supplementary angles in the diagram. Then, classify each angle as *acute, right,* or *obtuse.*

   - For each parallelogram, find the measures of the angles formed by extending two adjacent sides through their common vertex.

   a.   **b.**

19. While shopping for sneakers, Ling finds two pairs she likes. One pair costs $55 and the other costs $165. She makes the following statements about the prices.

   "The expensive sneakers cost $110 more than the cheaper sneakers."

   "The cost of the expensive sneakers is 300% of the cost of the cheaper sneakers."

   "The cheaper sneakers are $\frac{1}{3}$ the cost of the expensive sneakers."

   a. Are all her statements accurate? Explain.

   b. How are the comparison methods Ling uses like the methods you use to compare the sizes and shapes of similar figures?

   c. Which statements are appropriate for comparing the size and shape of an image to the original figure? Explain.

Extensions

20. A movie projector that is 6 feet away from a large screen shows a rectangular picture that is 3 feet wide and 2 feet high.

    a. Suppose the projector is moved to a point 12 feet from the screen. What size will the picture be (width, height, and area)?

    b. Suppose the projector is moved to a point 9 feet from the screen. What size will the picture be (width, height, and area)?

21. Amy's friend gave her a picture from Field Day. The picture is 3 in. by 2 in. Amy has a picture frame that is 6 in. by 4 in. She wants the photo to fit in the frame exactly. What percent enlargement does she need to make?

22. Make a three-band stretcher by tying three rubber bands together. Use this stretcher to enlarge the "Super Sleuth" drawing from Problem 1.1.

    a. How does the shape of the image compare to the shape of the original figure?

    b. How do the lengths of the segments in the two figures compare?

    c. How do the areas of the two figures compare?

    d. How do the distances from *P* compare?

23. Suppose you enlarge some triangles and squares with a two-band stretcher. You use an anchor point inside the original figure, as shown in the sketches below.

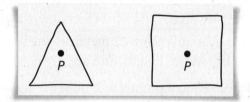

  a. In each case, how do the shape and position of the image compare to the shape and position of the original?

  b. What relationships do you expect to find among the side lengths, angle measures, perimeters, and areas of the figures, and the distances from P?

  c. Test your ideas with larger copies of the given shapes. Make sure the shortest distance from the anchor point to any side of a shape is at least one band length.

24. Suppose you make a stretcher with two different-sized rubber bands. Suppose the band attached to the anchor point is twice as long as the band attached to the pencil.

  a. If you used the stretcher to enlarge polygons, what relationships would you expect to find among the side lengths, angle measures, perimeters, and areas of the figures?

  b. Test your ideas with copies of some basic geometric shapes.

Mathematical Reflections

In this Investigation, you solved problems that involved enlarging (stretching) and reducing (shrinking) figures. You used rubber-band stretchers and copy machines to make scale drawings. The following questions will help you summarize what you have learned.

Think about these questions. Discuss your ideas with other students and your teacher. Then write a summary of your findings in your notebook.

1. a. **When** you enlarge or reduce a figure, what features stay the same?

    b. **When** you enlarge or reduce a figure, what features change?

2. Rubber-band stretchers, copy machines, and projectors all make images that are similar to the original shapes. **What** does it mean for two shapes to be similar? Complete the sentence below.

    "Two geometric shapes are similar when . . ."

Common Core Mathematical Practices

As you worked on the Problems in this Investigation, you used prior knowledge to make sense of them. You also applied Mathematical Practices to solve the Problems. Think back over your work, the ways you thought about the Problems, and how you used Mathematical Practices.

Tori described her thoughts in the following way:

In Problem 1.1, we had to describe how our original figure and the new image were alike and different. We had to compare the general shapes of the figures, the lengths of the line segments, the areas and perimeters, the angles, and the distance of each figure from a point.

Since our rubber band stretchers produced rough images, we used the edges of a piece of paper to make estimates of the lengths. Some other groups used rulers. To compare angle sizes, we used tracing paper to copy an angle. We compared this angle with a corresponding angle in the image.

Common Core Standards for Mathematical Practice
MP5 Use appropriate tools strategically

- What other Mathematical Practices can you identify in Tori's reasoning?

- Describe a Mathematical Practice that you and your classmates used to solve a different Problem in this Investigation.

Similar Figures

Zack and Marta want to design a computer game that involves several animated characters. They ask Marta's uncle, Carlos, a programmer for a video game company, about computer animation.

Carlos explains that the computer screen can be thought of as a grid made up of thousands of tiny points, called pixels. To animate a figure, you need to enter the coordinates of key points on the figure. The computer uses these points to draw the figure in different positions.

Each of the tiny dots on this screen is a *pixel*, which is a shortened form of "picture element."

Common Core State Standards

7.RP.A.2b Identify the constant of proportionality (unit rate) in tables, graphs, equations, diagrams, and verbal descriptions of proportional relationships.

7.G.A.1 Solve problems involving scale drawings of geometric figures, including computing actual lengths and areas from a scale drawing and reproducing a scale drawing at a different scale.

7.G.B.6 Solve real-world and mathematical problems involving area, volume and surface area of two- and three-dimensional objects composed of triangles, quadrilaterals, polygons, cubes, and right prisms.

Also 7.RP.A.2, 7.RP.A.2a and essential for 7.EE.B.4, 7.EE.B.4a

Sometimes the figures in a computer game need to change size. A computer can make a figure larger or smaller. You can give it a rule for finding key points on the new figure, using key points from the original figure.

Did You Know?

You can make figures and then rotate, slide, flip, stretch, and copy them using a computer graphics program. There are two basic kinds of graphics programs. Paint programs make images out of pixels. Draw programs make images out of lines that are drawn from mathematical equations.

The images you make in a graphics program are displayed on the computer screen. A beam of electrons activates a chemical in the screen, called phosphor, to make the images appear on your screen. If you have a laptop computer with a liquid crystal screen, an electric current makes the images appear on the screen.

2.1 Drawing Wumps
Making Similar Figures

Zack and Marta's computer game involves a family called the Wumps. The members of the Wump family are various sizes, but they all have the same shape. That is, they are *similar*. Mug Wump is the game's main character. By enlarging or reducing Mug, a player can transform him into other Wump family members.

Zack and Marta experiment with enlarging and reducing figures on a coordinate grid. First, Zack draws Mug Wump on graph paper. Then, he labels the key points from A to X and lists the coordinates for each point. Marta writes the rules that will change Mug's size.

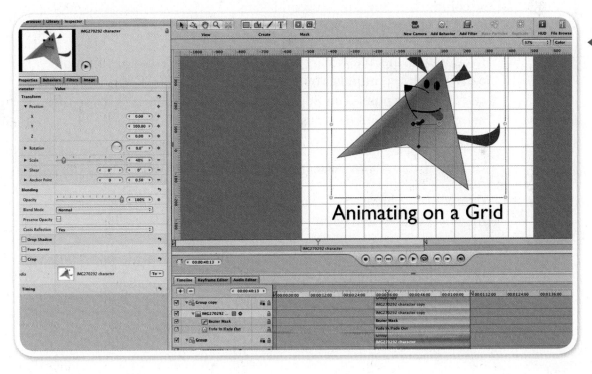

Problem 2.1

Marta tries several rules for transforming Mug into different sizes. At first glance, all the new characters look like Mug. They look like they might be mathematically similar to Mug. Some of the new characters are quite different, however. They are not mathematically similar to Mug.

A To draw Mug on a coordinate graph, refer to the "Mug Wump" column in the table on the next page.

- For Parts 1–3 of the figure, plot the points in order. Connect them as you go along.

- For Part 4, plot the two points, but do not connect them.

- When you are finished, describe Mug's shape.

B Use the columns for Zug, Lug, Bug, and Glug.

   1. Use the given rule to find the coordinates of the points.

      For example, the rule for Zug is $(2x, 2y)$. This means that you multiply each of Mug's coordinates by 2. Point A on Mug is $(0, 1)$, so the corresponding point A on Zug is $(0, 2)$. Point B on Mug is $(2, 1)$, so the corresponding point B on Zug is $(4, 2)$.

   2. Draw Zug, Lug, Bug, and Glug on separate coordinate planes. Plot and connect the points for each figure just as you did to draw Mug.

C **1.** Compare the characters to Mug. Which are the impostors (*not* members of the Wump family)?

   2. What things are the same about Mug and the others?

   3. What things are different about the five characters?

A C E Homework starts on page 36.

Coordinates of Game Characters

Point	Mug Wump (x, y)	Zug (2x, 2y)	Lug (3x, y)	Bug (3x, 3y)	Glug (x, 3y)
Rule					
	Part 1				
A	(0, 1)	(0, 2)	▪	▪	▪
B	(2, 1)	(4, 2)	▪	▪	▪
C	(2, 0)	▪	▪	▪	▪
D	(3, 0)	▪	▪	▪	▪
E	(3, 1)	▪	▪	▪	▪
F	(5, 1)	▪	▪	▪	▪
G	(5, 0)	▪	▪	▪	▪
H	(6, 0)	▪	▪	▪	▪
I	(6, 1)	▪	▪	▪	▪
J	(8, 1)	▪	▪	▪	▪
K	(6, 7)	▪	▪	▪	▪
L	(2, 7)	▪	▪	▪	▪
M	(0, 1)	▪	▪	▪	▪
	Part 2 (Start Over)				
N	(2, 2)	▪	▪	▪	▪
O	(6, 2)	▪	▪	▪	▪
P	(6, 3)	▪	▪	▪	▪
Q	(2, 3)	▪	▪	▪	▪
R	(2, 2)	▪	▪	▪	▪
	Part 3 (Start Over)				
S	(3, 4)	▪	▪	▪	▪
T	(4, 5)	▪	▪	▪	▪
U	(5, 4)	▪	▪	▪	▪
V	(3, 4)	▪	▪	▪	▪
	Part 4 (Start Over)				
W	(2, 5) (make a dot)	▪	▪	▪	▪
X	(6, 5) (make a dot)	▪	▪	▪	▪

2.2 Hats Off to the Wumps
Changing a Figure's Size and Location

Zack experiments with multiplying Mug's coordinates by different whole numbers to make other characters. Marta asks her uncle how multiplying the coordinates by a decimal or adding numbers to or subtracting numbers from each coordinate will affect Mug's shape. He gives her a sketch for a new shape (a hat for Mug) and some rules to try.

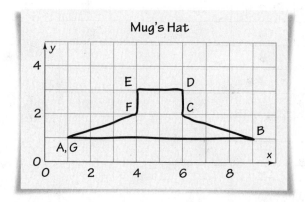

Mug's Hat

- Which rules will produce similar hats?

- How can you use a rule to predict side lengths of the image?

Problem 2.2

A Look at the rules for Hats 1 to 5 in the table. Before you find any coordinates, predict how each rule will change Mug's hat.

Rules for Mug's Hat

Point	Mug's Hat	Hat 1	Hat 2	Hat 3	Hat 4	Hat 5
	(x, y)	$(x + 2, y + 3)$	$(x - 1, y + 4)$	$(x + 2, 3y)$	$(0.5x, 0.5y)$	$(2x, 3y)$
A	(1, 1)	■	■	■	■	■
B	(9, 1)	■	■	■	■	■
C	■	■	■	■	■	■
D	■	■	■	■	■	■
E	■	■	■	■	■	■
F	■	■	■	■	■	■
G	■	■	■	■	■	■

B Copy and complete the table.

   1. Give the coordinates of Mug's hat and the five other hats.

   2. Plot each new hat on a separate coordinate grid and connect each point as you go.

C **1.** Compare the angles and side lengths of the hats.

   2. Which hats are similar to Mug's hat? Explain why.

D Write rules that will make hats similar to Mug's in each of these ways.

   1. The side lengths are one third as long as Mug's.

   2. The side lengths are 1.5 times as long as Mug's.

   3. The hat is the same size as Mug's, but has moved right 1 unit and up 5 units.

E Write a rule that makes a hat that is *not* similar to Mug's.

A C E Homework starts on page 36.

2.3 Mouthing Off and Nosing Around
Scale Factors

 How did you decide which of the computer game characters were members of the Wump family? How did you decide which were impostors?

- In general, how can you decide whether or not two shapes are similar?

You have experimented with rubber-band stretchers, copiers, and coordinate plots. Your experiments suggest that for two figures to be **similar,** there must be the following correspondence between the figures.

- The side lengths of one figure are multiplied by the same number to get the corresponding side lengths in the second figure.

- Corresponding angles are the same size.

● The **scale factor** is the number that the side lengths of one figure can be multiplied by to give the corresponding side lengths of the other figure.

The rectangles below are similar. The scale factor from the smaller rectangle to the larger rectangle is 3.

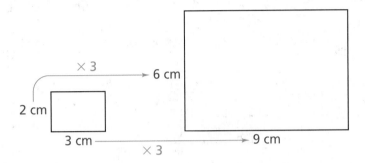

- What is the scale factor from the larger rectangle to the smaller rectangle? Explain how you found it.

Chicago Model City is a 1 : 600 scale model of the city. The buildings were made using a 3D printer. Each building is made of many thin layers of resin, hardened by a laser and then painted.

Problem 2.3

The diagram shows a collection of mouths (rectangles) and noses (triangles). Some are from the Wump family. Others are from impostors.

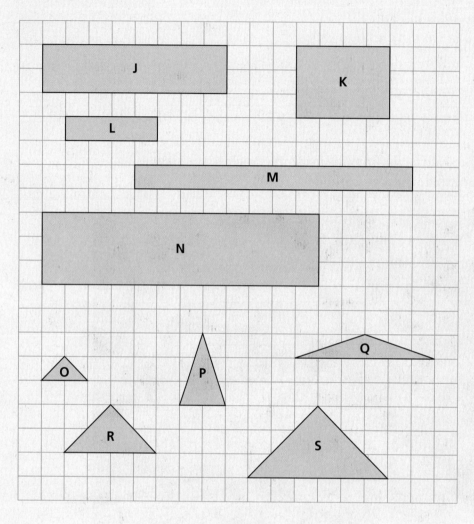

continued

Use the rectangles on the previous page.

A **1.** Which pairs of rectangles are similar? Explain how you know.

 2. For each pair of similar rectangles, find the scale factor and the perimeter and area of each rectangle.

 3. Describe the relationship between the perimeters of two similar rectangles and the scale factor.

 4. Describe the relationship between the areas of two similar rectangles and the scale factor.

B **1.** Which pairs of triangles are similar? Explain how you know.

 2. For each pair of similar triangles, find the scale factor. Then find the area of each triangle.

 3. Does the same relationship between the scale factor of similar rectangles and their area apply for similar triangles? Explain.

 4. Draw three right triangles such that exactly two of the right triangles are similar. Explain how each triangle is similar or not similar to the other two.

C **1.** After studying the mouths in the diagram, Marta and Zack agree that Rectangles J and L are similar. Marta says the scale factor is 2. Zack says it is 0.5. Is either of them correct? How would you describe the scale factor so there is no confusion?

 2. Explain how to find the scale factor from a figure to a similar figure.

 3. Does the scale factor change the angle sizes? Explain.

 4. You have used rubber bands and coordinate graphs to make similar figures. How does the scale factor show up in each of these methods?

 Homework starts on page 36.

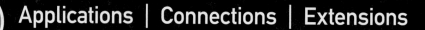
Applications

1. The table below gives key coordinates for drawing Mug Wump's mouth and nose. It also gives rules for finding the corresponding points for four other characters—some members of the Wump family and some impostors.

Coordinates of Characters

Rule	Mug Wump (x, y)	Glum (1.5x, 1.5y)	Sum (3x, 2y)	Tum (4x, 4y)	Crum (2x, y)
Point	Mouth				
M	(2, 2)	▪	▪	▪	▪
N	(6, 2)	▪	▪	▪	▪
O	(6, 3)	▪	▪	▪	▪
P	(2, 3)	▪	▪	▪	▪
Q	(2, 2) (connect Q to M)	▪	▪	▪	▪
	Nose (Start Over)				
R	(3, 4)	▪	▪	▪	▪
S	(4, 5)	▪	▪	▪	▪
T	(5, 4)	▪	▪	▪	▪
U	(3, 4) (connect U to R)	▪	▪	▪	▪

a. Before you find the coordinates or plot points, predict which characters are the impostors.

b. Copy and complete the table. Then, plot the figures on grid paper. Label each figure.

c. Which of the new characters (Glum, Sum, Tum, and Crum) are members of the Wump family? Which are impostors?

d. Choose one of the new Wumps. How do the mouth and nose measurements (side lengths, perimeter, area, angle measures) compare with those of Mug Wump?

e. Choose one of the impostors. What are the dimensions of this impostor's mouth and nose? How do the mouth and nose measurements compare with those of Mug Wump?

f. Do your findings in parts (b)–(e) support your prediction from part (a)? Explain.

2. a. Design a Mug-like character of your own on grid paper. Give your character eyes, a nose, and a mouth.

  b. Give coordinates so that someone else could draw your character.

  c. Write a rule for finding coordinates of a member of your character's family. Check your rule by plotting the figure.

  d. Write a rule for finding the coordinates of an impostor. Check your rule by plotting the figure.

3. a. On grid paper, draw triangle ABC with vertex coordinates $A(0, 2)$, $B(6, 2)$, and $C(4, 4)$.

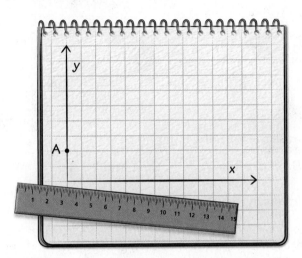

  b. Apply the rule $(1.5x, 1.5y)$ to the vertices of triangle ABC to get triangle PQR. Compare the corresponding measurements (side lengths, perimeters, areas, area, angle measures) of the two triangles.

  c. Apply the rule $(2x, 0.5y)$ to the vertices of triangle ABC to get triangle FGH. Compare the corresponding measurements (side lengths, perimeters, areas, angle measures) of the two triangles.

  d. Which triangle, PQR or FGH, seems similar to triangle ABC? Why?

4. a. On grid paper, draw parallelogram $ABCD$ with vertex coordinates $A(0, 2)$, $B(6, 2)$, $C(8, 6)$, and $D(2, 6)$.

  b. Write a rule to find the vertex coordinates of a parallelogram $PQRS$ that is larger than, but similar to, $ABCD$. Test your rule to see if it works.

  c. Write a rule to find the vertex coordinates of a parallelogram $TUVW$ that is smaller than, but similar to, $ABCD$. Test your rule to see if it works.

For Exercises 5 and 6, study the size and shape of the polygons below.

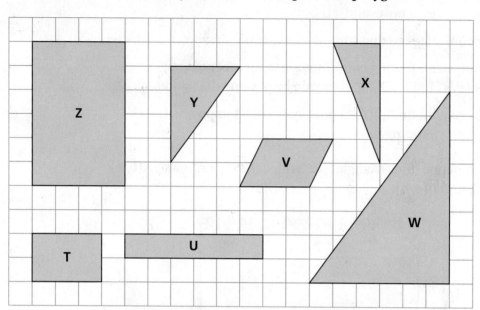

5. **Multiple Choice** Choose the pair of similar figures.

   A. Z and Y   **B.** V and T   **C.** X and Y   **D.** Y and W

6. Find another pair of similar figures. Explain your reasoning.

7. Copy the figures below accurately onto your own grid paper.

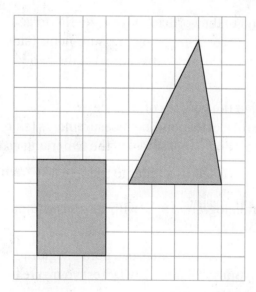

   a. Draw a figure similar, but not identical, to the rectangle.

   b. Draw a figure similar, but not identical, to the triangle.

   c. How do you know your scale drawings are similar to the given figures?

8. The diagram below shows two similar polygons.

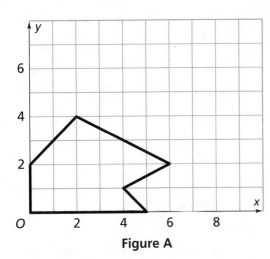

Figure A

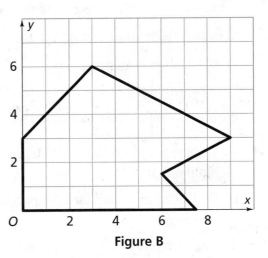

Figure B

a. Write a rule for finding the coordinates of a point on Figure B from the corresponding point on Figure A.

b. Write a rule for finding the coordinates of a point on Figure A from the corresponding point on Figure B.

c. i. What is the scale factor from Figure A to Figure B?

    ii. Use the scale factor to describe how the perimeter and area of Figure B are related to the perimeter and area of Figure A.

d. i. What is the scale factor from Figure B to Figure A?

    ii. Use the scale factor to describe how the perimeter and area of Figure A are related to the perimeter and area of Figure B.

9. a. Suppose you make Figure C by applying the rule $(2x, 2y)$ to the points on Figure A from Exercise 8. Find the coordinates of the vertices of Figure C.

b. i. What is the scale factor from Figure A to Figure C?

    ii. Use the scale factor to describe how the perimeter and area of Figure C are related to the perimeter and area of Figure A.

c. i. What is the scale factor from Figure C to Figure A?

    ii. Use the scale factor to describe how the perimeter and area of Figure A are related to the perimeter and area of Figure C.

    iii. Write a coordinate rule of the form (mx, my) that can be used to find the coordinates of any point of Figure A from the corresponding points of Figure C.

10. What is the scale factor from an original figure to its image if the image is made using the given method?

a. a two-rubber-band stretcher

b. a copy machine with size factor 150%

c. a copy machine with size factor 250%

d. the coordinate rule $(0.75x, 0.75y)$

11. **a.** Use the polygons below. Which pairs of polygons are similar figures?

b. For each pair of similar figures, list corresponding sides and angles.

c. For each pair of similar figures, find the scale factor that relates side lengths of the larger figure to the corresponding side lengths of the smaller figure.

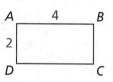

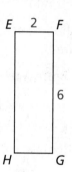

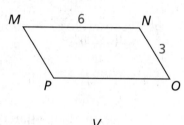

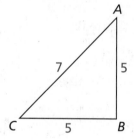

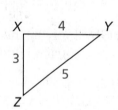

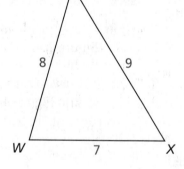

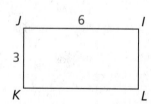

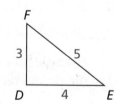

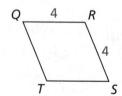

12. On grid paper, draw a rectangle with an area of 14 square centimeters. Label it *ABCD*.

    a. Write and use a coordinate rule that will make a rectangle similar to rectangle *ABCD* that is three times as long and three times as wide. Label it *EFGH*.

    b. How does the perimeter of rectangle *EFGH* compare to the perimeter of rectangle *ABCD*?

    c. How does the area of rectangle *EFGH* compare to the area of rectangle *ABCD*?

    d. How do your answers to parts (b) and (c) relate to the scale factor from rectangle *ABCD* to rectangle *EFGH*?

13. A student drew the figures below. The student says the two shapes are similar because there is a common scale factor for all of the sides. The sides of the figure on the right are twice as long as those of the figure on the left. What do you say to the student to explain why the figures are *not* similar?

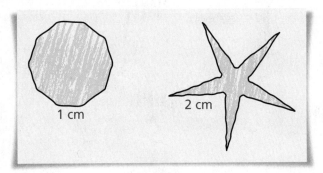

Connections

For Exercises 14 and 15, the rule $(x, \frac{3}{4}y)$ is applied to a polygon.

14. Is the image similar to the original polygon? Explain.

15. Each of the following points is on the original polygon. Find the coordinates of each corresponding point on the image.

    a. (6, 8)   **b.** (9, 8)   **c.** $\left(\frac{3}{2}, \frac{4}{3}\right)$

Multiple Choice For Exercises 16 and 17, what is the percent reduction or enlargement that will result if the rule is applied to a figure on a coordinate grid?

16. $(1.5x, 1.5y)$

    A. 150%   **B.** 15%   **C.** 1.5%   **D.** None of these

17. $(0.7x, 0.7y)$

    F. 700%   **G.** 7%   **H.** 0.7%   **J.** None of these

18. The rule $\left(x + \frac{2}{3}, y - \frac{3}{4}\right)$ is applied to a polygon. For each vertex below of the polygon, find the coordinates of the corresponding vertex on the image.

    a. $(5, 3)$ **b.** $\left(\frac{1}{6}, \frac{11}{12}\right)$ **c.** $\left(\frac{9}{12}, \frac{4}{5}\right)$

19. An accurate map is a scale drawing of the place it represents. Below is a map of South Africa.

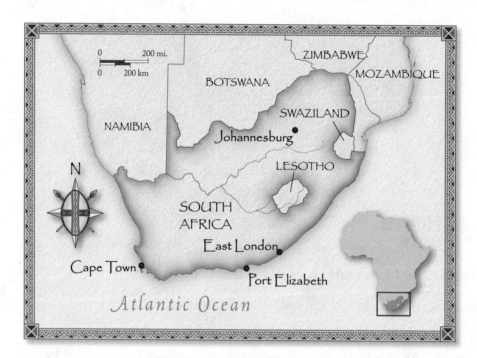

    a. Use the scale to estimate the distance from Cape Town to Port Elizabeth.

    b. Use the scale to estimate the distance from Johannesburg to East London.

    c. What is the relationship between the scale for the map and a "scale factor"?

Find each quotient.

20. $\frac{1}{2} \div \frac{1}{4}$

21. $\frac{1}{4} \div \frac{1}{2}$

22. $\frac{3}{7} \div \frac{4}{7}$

23. $\frac{4}{7} \div \frac{3}{7}$

24. $\frac{3}{2} \div \frac{3}{5}$

25. $1\frac{1}{2} \div \frac{3}{8}$

26. At a bake sale, 0.72 of a pan of corn bread has not been sold. A serving is 0.04 of a pan.

    a. How many servings are left?

    b. Use a hundredths grid to show your reasoning.

27. Each pizza takes 0.3 of a large block of cheese. Charlie has 0.8 of a block of cheese left.

    a. How many pizzas can he make?

    b. Use a diagram to show your reasoning.

28. a. What part of the grid below is shaded?

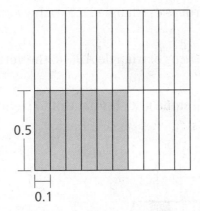

    b. The grid shows the part of a pan of spinach appetizers remaining. How many servings are left if a serving is 0.04?

    c. Draw a picture to confirm your answer to part (b).

Extensions

29. Select a drawing of a comic strip character from a newspaper or magazine. Draw a grid over the figure or tape a transparent grid on top of the figure. Identify key points on the figure and then enlarge it using each of these rules. Which figures are similar? Explain.

    a. $(2x, 2y)$ **b.** $(x, 2y)$ **c.** $(2x, y)$

30. Suppose you use the rule $(3x + 1, 3y - 4)$ to transform Mug Wump into a new figure.

    a. How will the angle measures in the new figure compare to corresponding angle measures in Mug?

    b. How will the side lengths of the new figure compare to corresponding side lengths of Mug?

    c. How will the area and perimeter of this new figure compare to the area and perimeter of Mug?

31. The vertices of three similar triangles are given.

    • triangle *ABC*: $A(1, 2)$, $B(4, 3)$, $C(2, 5)$

    • triangle *DEF*: $D(3, 6)$, $E(12, 9)$, $F(6, 15)$

    • triangle *GHI*: $G(5, 9)$, $H(14, 12)$, $I(8, 18)$

    a. Find a rule that changes the vertices of triangle *ABC* to the vertices of triangle *DEF*.

    b. Find a rule that changes the vertices of triangle *DEF* to the vertices of triangle *GHI*.

    c. Find a rule that changes the vertices of triangle *ABC* to the vertices of triangle *GHI*.

32. If you drew Mug and his hat on the same grid, his hat would be at his feet instead of on his head.

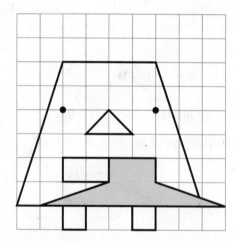

    a. Write a rule that puts Mug's hat centered on his head.

    b. Write a rule that changes Mug's hat to fit Zug and puts the hat on Zug's head.

    c. Write a rule that changes Mug's hat to fit Lug and puts the hat on Lug's head.

33. Films are sometimes modified to fit a TV screen. Find out what that means. What exactly is modified? If Mug is in a movie, is he still a Wump when you see the video on TV?

34. The diagram below shows Mug Wump drawn on a coordinate grid. Use this diagram to answer the questions on the next page.

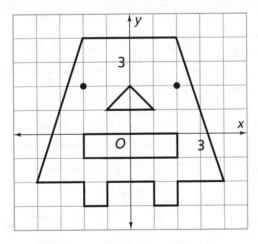

a. Use the diagram on the previous page. Complete the first column of a table like the one shown to record coordinates of key points needed to draw Mug. (You will need to determine the number of points needed for each body part.)

b. Suppose you make scale drawings with rules $(2x, 2y)$ and $(-2x, -2y)$. Complete the table to give coordinates for the images of Mug.

c. On graph paper, plot the images of Mug Wump produced by the new sets of coordinates in part (b).

d. Compare the length, width, and area of Mug's mouth to those of the figures drawn in part (c). Explain how you could have predicted those results by studying the coordinate rules for the drawings.

Coordinates for Mug and Variations

Rule	(x, y)	$(2x, 2y)$	$(-2x, -2y)$
Head Outline	$(-4, -2)$	■	■
	$(-2, -2)$	■	■
	$(-2, 3)$	■	■
	■	■	■
	■	■	■
Nose	$(-1, 1)$	■	■
	■	■	■
	■	■	■
Mouth	$(-2, -1)$	■	■
	■	■	■
	■	■	■
	■	■	■
Eyes	$(-2, 2)$	■	■
	■	■	■

35. Explain how each rule changes the original shape, size, and location of Mug Wump.

a. $(-x, y)$

b. $(x, -y)$

c. $(-0.5x, -0.5y)$

d. $(-0.5x, y)$

e. $(-3x, -3y)$

f. $(3x + 5, -3y - 4)$

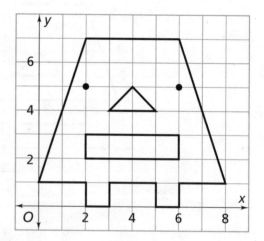

36. The diagram below shows Mug Wump drawn at the center of a coordinate grid and in four other positions.

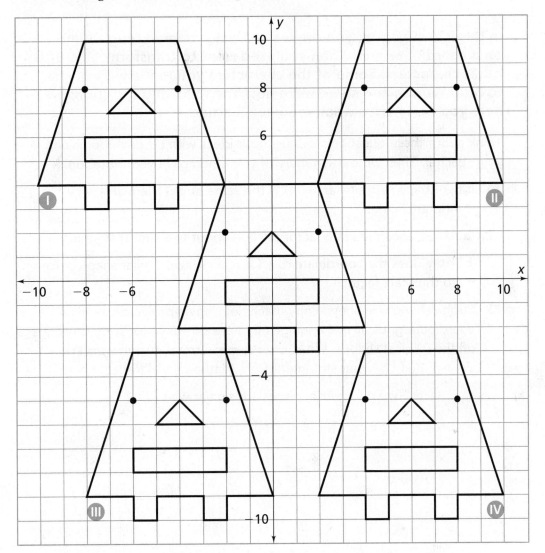

a. Find a sequence of coordinates to draw Mug's body at the center of the grid. Make a table to keep track of the points. For parts (b) and (c) below, use this Mug as the original Mug.

b. You can write a coordinate rule to describe the movement of points from one location to another. For example, the coordinate rule $(x - 2, y + 3)$ moves a point (x, y) to the left 2 units and up 3 units from its original location. Which of the other drawings is produced by the coordinate rule $(x + 6, y - 7)$?

c. Find coordinate rules for moving the original Mug to the other positions on the grid.

Mathematical Reflections

In this Investigation, you drew a character named Mug Wump on a coordinate grid. Then you used rules to transform Mug into other characters. Some of the characters you made were similar to Mug Wump, and some were not. The following questions will help you summarize what you have learned.

Think about these questions. Discuss your ideas with other students and your teacher. Then write a summary of your findings in your notebook.

1. If two shapes are similar, **what** is the same about them and what is different?

2. **a. What** does the scale factor tell you about two similar shapes?

   b. How does the coordinate rule for making two similar shapes relate to the scale factor?

3. Rubber-band stretchers, copy machines, movie projectors, and coordinate grids all make images that are similar to (or scale drawings of) the original shapes. **What** does it mean to say two shapes are similar? Build on your statement from Mathematical Reflection 1:

   "Two geometric shapes are similar when . . ."

Common Core Mathematical Practices

As you worked on the Problems in this Investigation, you used prior knowledge to make sense of them. You also applied Mathematical Practices to solve the Problems. Think back over your work, the ways you thought about the Problems, and how you used Mathematical Practices.

Hector described his thoughts in the following way:

> We noticed a relationship between the areas of similar figures. For example, in Problem 2.3, Question A, the scale factor from Rectangle L to Rectangle N is 3, and 9 of Rectangle L fit into Rectangle N. Therefore, the scale factor for the area is 3×3. This is the same as the "square of the scale factor" of the sides: 3^2.
>
> The same rule works for triangles. This confirms the claims we made about areas of triangles and rectangles in Problem 1.2.
>
> ....
>
> **Common Core Standards for Mathematical Practice**
> **MP7** Look for and make use of structure

- What other Mathematical Practices can you identify in Hector's reasoning?

- Describe a Mathematical Practice that you and your classmates used to solve a different Problem in this Investigation.

Investigation 3

Scaling Perimeter and Area

In *Shapes and Designs*, you learned that some polygons fit together to cover, or tile, a flat surface. For example, the surface of a honeycomb has a pattern of regular hexagons. Many bathroom and kitchen floors are covered with a pattern of square tiles. These patterns of polygons that fit together are called *tessellations*.

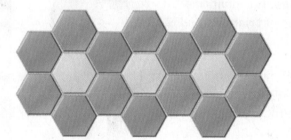

Common Core State Standards

7.RP.A.2b Identify the constant of proportionality . . . in diagrams and verbal descriptions of proportional relationships.

7.G.A.1 Solve problems involving scale drawings of geometric figures, including computing actual lengths and areas from a scale drawing and reproducing a scale drawing at a different scale.

7.G.A.2 Draw (freehand, with ruler and protractor, and with technology) geometric shapes with given conditions. Focus on constructing triangles from three measures of angles or sides . . .

7.G.B.6 Solve real-world and mathematical problems involving area, volume, and surface area of two- and three-dimensional objects composed of triangles, quadrilaterals, polygons, cubes, and right prisms.

Also 7.RP.A.2, 7.RP.A.2a, and essential for 7.RP.A.3, 7.EE.B.4, 7.EE.B.4a

Look closely at the pattern of squares on the previous page. You can see that the large square consists of nine small squares. The large square is similar to each of the nine small squares. The large square has sides formed by the sides of three small squares, so the scale factor from the small square to the large square is 3.

You can also put four small squares together to make a four-tile square. This four-tile square is similar to both the large nine-tile square and the small single-tile square. The scale factor from the single-tile square to the four-tile square is 2. The scale factor from the four-tile square to the single-tile square is $\frac{1}{2}$.

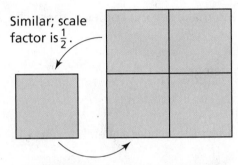

Similar; scale factor is $\frac{1}{2}$.

Similar; scale factor is 2.

No matter how closely you look at the hexagon pattern, however, you cannot find a large hexagon made up of similar smaller hexagons.

A shape is a **rep-tile** if you can put together *congruent* (same size and shape) copies of the shape to make a larger, similar shape. The congruent copies may be rotated in order to fit together. A square is a rep-tile, but a regular hexagon is not.

- Which quadrilaterals are rep-tiles?
- For those that are, how might you subdivide them into smaller, similar figures?

3.1 Rep-Tile Quadrilaterals
Forming Rep-Tiles With Similar Quadrilaterals

In this Problem, you will discover which rectangles and non-rectangular quadrilaterals are rep-tiles.

Problem 3.1

Sketch or use your Shapes Set to make several copies of these shapes:

- a non-square rectangle
- a non-rectangular parallelogram
- a trapezoid

A Which of these shapes is a rep-tile? Make a sketch to show how the copies fit together.

B Look at your sketches from Question A.

1. What is the scale factor from the original figure to the larger figure? Explain your reasoning.

2. How does the perimeter of the larger figure relate to the perimeter of the original figure?

3. How does the area of the larger figure relate to the area of the original figure?

C 1. Extend the rep-tile patterns you drew for Question A. Do this by sketching additional copies of the original figure to make even larger figures that are similar to the original. Show how the copies fit together.

2. Find the scale factor from each original figure to each new figure. Explain your reasoning.

3. What do the scale factors tell you about the corresponding side lengths, perimeters, angles, and areas?

ACE Homework starts on page 60.

3.2 Rep-Tile Triangles
Forming Rep-Tiles With Similar Triangles

Rep-tiles must tessellate, but not every shape that tessellates is a rep-tile.

- Are the birds in the tessellation below rep-tiles?

In Problem 3.1, you determined which quadrilaterals are rep-tiles. In this Problem, you will investigate which triangles are rep-tiles.

> ❓ Which types of triangles are rep-tiles?

Did You Know?

Mathematicians and scientists are very interested in rep-tiles. They share many properties with strange, newly discovered, crystal-like figures called quasicrystals. Quasicrystals do not have the translational symmetry of ordinary crystals, but they have other properties that ordinary crystals do not have. Scientists are currently researching the properties of quasicrystals and why they work. Quasicrystals are used to insulate wires and to coat mechanical parts to prevent erosion and wear. Quasicrystals even work well as a coating for non-stick frying pans!

Problem 3.2

Sketch or use your Shapes Set to make several copies of these shapes:

- a right triangle
- an isosceles triangle
- a scalene triangle

A Which of these triangles is a rep-tile? Make a sketch to show how copies of the original figure fit together to make a larger, similar triangle.

B Look at your sketches from Question A.

    1. What is the scale factor from each original triangle to each larger triangle? Explain your reasoning.

    2. How is the perimeter of the larger triangle related to the perimeter of the original?

    3. How is the area of the larger triangle related to the area of the original?

C **1.** Extend the rep-tile patterns you made in Question A. Do this by sketching additional copies of the original triangle to make even larger triangles that are similar to the original. Show how the copies fit together.

    2. Find the scale factor from each original triangle to each new triangle.

    3. What do the scale factors tell you about the corresponding side lengths, perimeters, angles, and areas?

Problem **3.2** *continued*

D Study the rep-tile patterns you sketched for Questions A and C. Copy each of the triangles below. Then divide each triangle into four or more smaller, similar triangles.

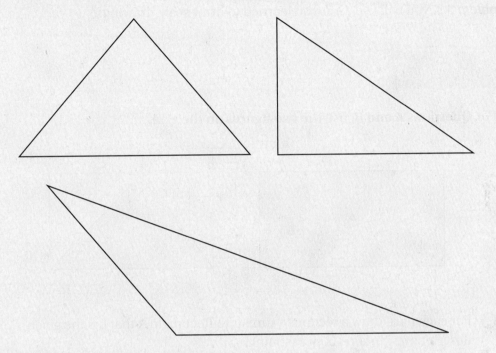

E **1.** Suppose you are given a rectangle or triangle rep-tile and a scale factor of 5. How many copies of your rep-tile would be needed to make the scale copy? Explain your reasoning.

2. It takes nine copies of a certain rep-tile to make a similar figure. What is the scale factor between the original rep-tile and the image? Explain.

3. Tomoko claims that all triangles are rep-tiles. Is this true? Explain.

ACE Homework starts on page 60.

3.3 Designing Under Constraints
Scale Factors and Similar Shapes

The scale factor from one figure to a similar figure gives you information about how the side lengths, perimeters, and areas of the figures are related. In Problem 3.3, you will use what you learned to draw scale drawings.

Problem **3.3**

For Questions A and B, use the two figures on the grid.

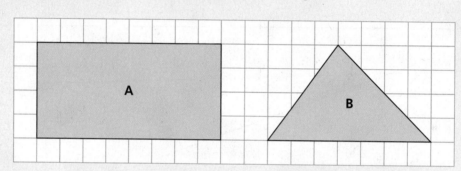

A For each part, draw a rectangle similar to Rectangle A that fits the given description. Explain your reasoning.

   1. The scale factor from Rectangle A to the new rectangle is 2.5.

   2. The area of the new rectangle is $\frac{1}{4}$ the area of Rectangle A.

   3. The perimeter of the new rectangle is three times the perimeter of Rectangle A.

B For each part, draw a triangle similar to Triangle B that fits the given description. Explain your reasoning.

   1. The area of the new triangle is 16 times the area of Triangle B.

   2. The scale factor from Triangle B to the new triangle is $\frac{1}{2}$.

Problem **3.3** *continued*

C **1.** Rectangles *ABCD* and *EFGH* are similar. Find the length of side *AD*. Explain how you found the length.

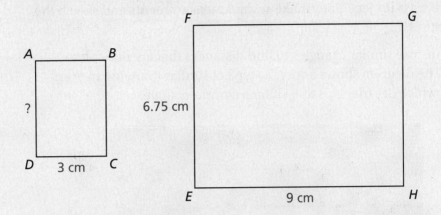

2. Triangles *ABC* and *DEF* are similar. Find the missing side lengths and angle measures. Explain.

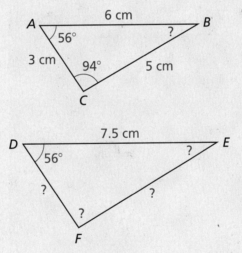

A C E Homework starts on page 60.

3.4 Out of Reach
Finding Lengths With Similar Triangles

Durell, Angie, and Tonya are designing a triangular boardwalk that crosses a river for a class project. They make several measurements and sketch the diagram below.

The students use similar triangles to find distances that are difficult to measure. The diagram shows a specific type of similar triangles, **nested triangles,** which are triangles that share a common angle.

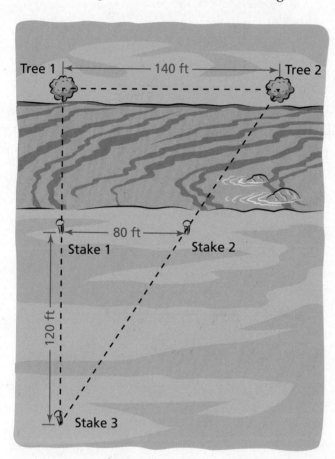

- The angles that look like right angles are right angles. How are the angles in the smaller triangle related to the angles in the larger triangle?

- Durell claims that he can use rep-tiles to show that the smaller right triangle is similar to the larger right triangle. Is he correct?

Two triangles are similar if corresponding angles are congruent. In a later Unit, you will prove this fact. For now, we will assume that it is true.

Problem 3.4

A The triangles in the diagram on the previous page are similar. What is the distance across the river from Stake 1 to Tree 1? Explain your reasoning.

B Describe the relationship between the perimeter of the smaller triangle and the perimeter of the larger triangle.

C The diagram on the previous page shows three stakes and two trees. In what order do you think Durell, Angie, and Tonya located the key points and measured the segments and angles? Explain your reasoning.

D Another group of students sketches a different diagram with similar triangles. They put their stakes in different places. Use the diagram below. Does the second group get the same measurement for the width of the river? Explain.

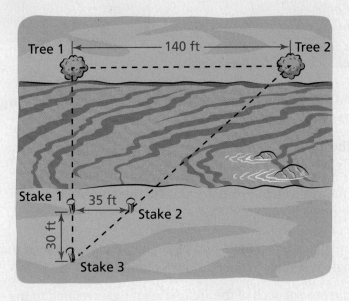

A C E Homework starts on page 60.

Applications

1. Look for rep-tile patterns in the designs below. For each design,

   • Decide whether the small quadrilaterals are similar to the large quadrilateral. Explain.

   • If the quadrilaterals are similar, give the scale factor from each small quadrilateral to the large quadrilateral.

   a.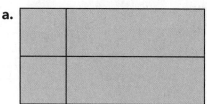
   b.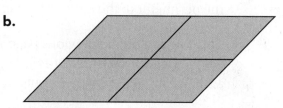

   c.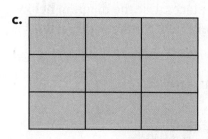
   d.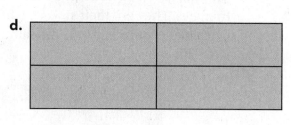

2. Suppose you put together nine copies of a rectangle to make a larger, similar rectangle.

   a. How is the area of the larger rectangle related to the area of the smaller rectangle?

   b. What is the scale factor from the smaller rectangle to the larger rectangle?

3. Suppose you divide a rectangle into 25 smaller rectangles such that each rectangle is similar to the original rectangle.

   a. How is the area of each of the smaller rectangles related to the area of the original rectangle?

   b. What is the scale factor from the original rectangle to each of the smaller rectangles?

4. Look for rep-tile patterns in the figures below.

- Tell whether the small triangles are similar to the large triangle. Explain.

- If the triangles are similar, give the scale factor from each small triangle to the large triangle.

a.

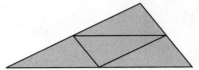

b.

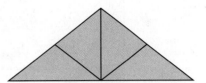

c.

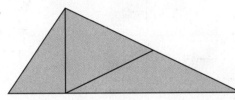

d.

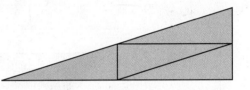

5. a. For rectangles E–G, give the length and width of a different, similar rectangle. Explain how you know the new rectangles are similar.

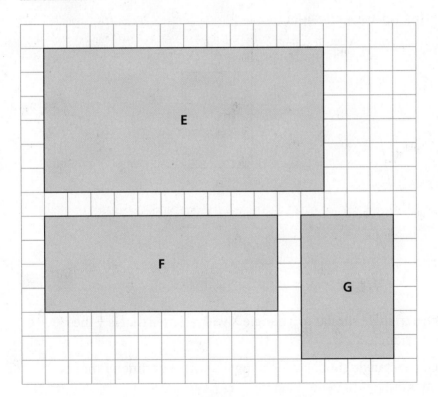

b. Give the scale factor from each original rectangle in part (a) to the similar rectangles you described. Explain what the scale factor tells you about the corresponding lengths, perimeters, and areas.

6. Copy polygons A–D onto grid paper. Draw line segments that divide each of the polygons into four congruent polygons that are similar to the original polygon.

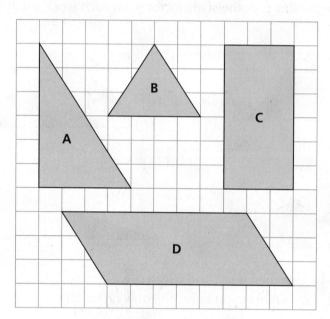

7. For parts (a)–(c), use grid paper.

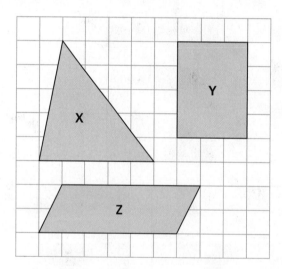

a. Sketch a triangle similar to Triangle X with an area that is $\frac{1}{4}$ the area of Triangle X.

b. Sketch a rectangle similar to Rectangle Y with a perimeter that is 0.5 times the perimeter of Rectangle Y.

c. Sketch a parallelogram similar to Parallelogram Z with side lengths that are 1.5 times the side lengths of Parallelogram Z.

8. Use the polygons below.

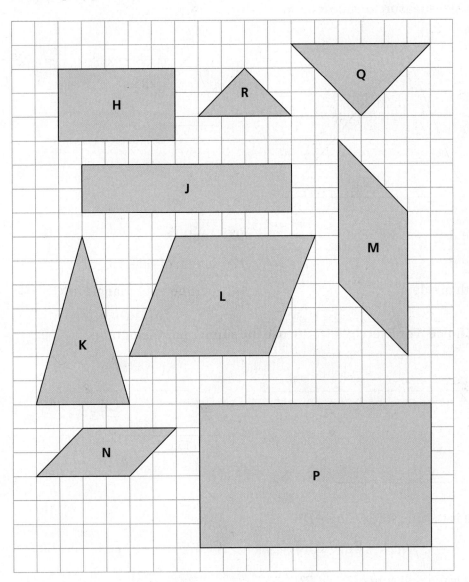

a. List pairs of similar shapes.

b. For each pair of similar shapes, find the scale factor from the smaller shape to the larger shape.

Triangle *ABC* is similar to triangle *PQR*. For Exercises 9–14, find the indicated angle measure or side length.

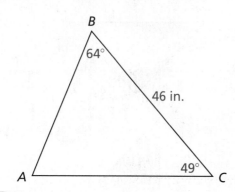

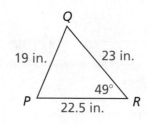

9. angle *A*

10. angle *Q*

11. angle *P*

12. length of side *AB*

13. length of side *AC*

14. perimeter of triangle *ABC*

Multiple Choice For Exercises 15–18, use the similar parallelograms below.

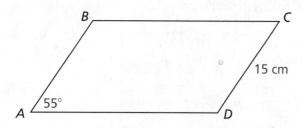

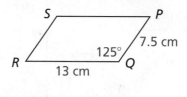

15. What is the measure of angle *D*?

    A. 55°   **B.** 97.5°   **C.** 125°   **D.** 135°

16. What is the measure of angle *R*?

    F. 55°   **G.** 97.5°   **H.** 125°   **J.** 135°

17. What is the measure of angle *S*?

    A. 55°   **B.** 97.5°   **C.** 125°   **D.** 135°

18. What is length of side *AB*?

    F. 3.75 cm   **G.** 13 cm   **H.** 15 cm   **J.** 26 cm

19. Suppose Rectangle B is similar to Rectangle A below. The scale factor from Rectangle A to Rectangle B is 4. What is the area of Rectangle B?

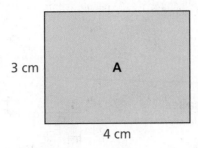

3 cm   A

4 cm

20. Suppose Rectangle E has an area of 9 square centimeters and Rectangle F has an area of 900 square centimeters. The two rectangles are similar. What is the scale factor from Rectangle E to Rectangle F?

21. Suppose Rectangles X and Y are similar. Rectangle X is 5 centimeters by 7 centimeters. The area of Rectangle Y is 140 square centimeters. What are the dimensions of Rectangle Y?

22. Anya and Jalen disagree about whether the two figures below are similar. Do you agree with Anya or with Jalen? Explain.

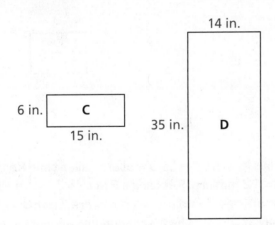

14 in.

6 in.   C

15 in.

35 in.   D

Anya's Reasoning

The two rectangles are not similar. The height of Rectangle D is almost 6 times the height of Rectangle C, but the widths are almost the same. Similar rectangles must have the same scale factor for the base and the height.

OR

Jalen's Reasoning

The two rectangles are similar. The scale factor from C to D is $\frac{7}{3}$. You can multiply the short side of C (the height) by to get 14 inches, which is the short side of D (the base). This scale factor also works for the long sides of the rectangles since $15 \times \frac{7}{3} = 35$.

23. Evan, Melanie, and Wyatt discuss whether the two figures at the right are similar. Do you agree with Evan, Melanie, or Wyatt? Explain.

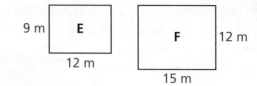

Evan's Reasoning

Rectangles E and F are similar because each shape has four right angles. Also, each rectangle has at least one side that is 12 meters long.

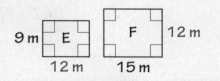

Melanie's Reasoning

The scale factor for the height from rectangle E to rectangle F is $\frac{12}{9}$, or $\frac{4}{3}$. The scale factor for the base is $\frac{15}{12}$, or $\frac{5}{4}$. $\frac{4}{3} \neq \frac{5}{4}$, so the rectangles are not similar.

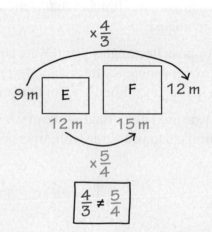

Wyatt's Reasoning

Rectangles E and F are similar. Rectangle F is 3 meters taller than Rectangle E since 9 meters + 3 meters = 12 meters. Rectangle F is also 3 meters wider than Rectangle E since 12 meters + 3 meters = 15 meters. Each dimension of Rectangle F is 3 meters greater than the corresponding dimension of Rectangle E, so the rectangles are similar.

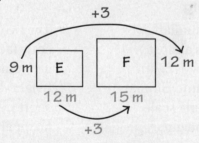

24. Janine, Trisha, and Jeff drew parallelograms that are similar to Parallelogram *P* below.

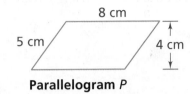

8 cm

5 cm

4 cm

Parallelogram *P*

Each student claims that the scale factor from *P* to the sketched parallelogram is 4. Are any of the students correct in their reasoning? Explain.

Janine's Method

I divided the original parallelogram into four similar parallelograms. Parallelogram *P* is four times as large as each of the new parallelograms.

Trisha's Method

I sketched four copies of parallelogram P. The shape has four times the area of parallelogram P.

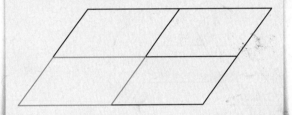

Jeff's Method

I wanted a scale factor of 4. The perimeter of the original shape is 26 centimeters. I drew a parallelogram with a perimeter of 4 × 26 centimeters = 104 centimeters.

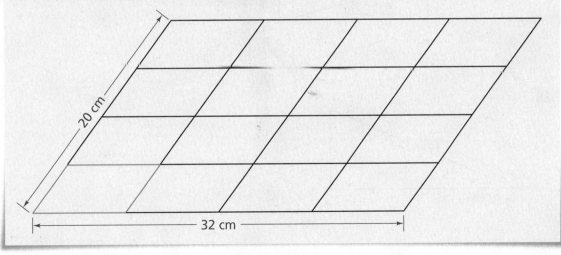

20 cm

32 cm

25. Judy lies on the ground 45 feet from her tent. Both the top of the tent and the top of a tall cliff are in her line of sight. Her tent is 10 feet tall. About how high is the cliff? Assume the two triangles are similar.

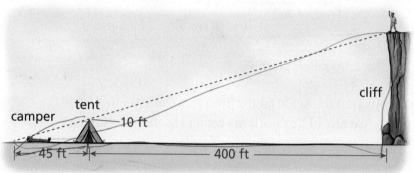

Not drawn to scale

For Exercises 26–28, each triangle has been subdivided into triangles that are similar to the original triangle. Copy each triangle and label as many side lengths as you can.

26.

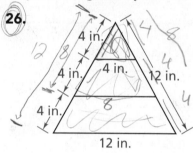

27.

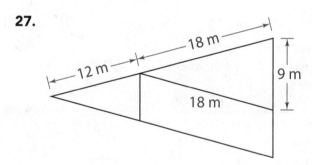

28.

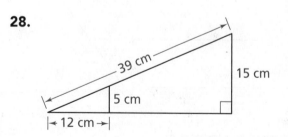

Connections

29. In the figure below, lines L_1 and L_2 are parallel.

a. Use what you know about parallel lines to find the measures of angles *a* through *g*.

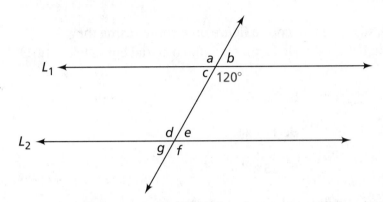

b. List all pairs of *supplementary* angles in the diagram.

30. For each of the following angle measures, find the measure of its supplementary angle.

a. 160°   **b.** 90°   **c.** $x°$

31. The right triangles below are similar.

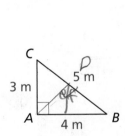
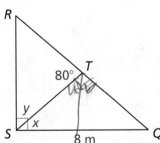

a. Find the length of side *RS*.

b. Find the length of side *RQ*.

c. The measure of angle *x* is about 40°. If the measure of angle *x* were exactly 40°, what would be the measure of angle *y*?

d. Use your answer from part (c) to find the measure of angle *R*. Explain how you can find the measure of angle *C*.

e. Angle *x* and angle *y* are *complementary angles*. Find two additional pairs of complementary angles in Triangles *ABC* and *QRS*.

32. For parts (a)–(f), find the number that makes the fractions equivalent.

  a. $\frac{1}{2} = \frac{3}{\blacksquare}$ b. $\frac{5}{6} = \frac{\blacksquare}{24}$

  c. $\frac{3}{4} = \frac{6}{\blacksquare}$ d. $\frac{8}{12} = \frac{2}{\blacksquare}$

  e. $\frac{3}{5} = \frac{\blacksquare}{100}$ f. $\frac{6}{4} = \frac{\blacksquare}{10}$

33. For parts (a)–(f), suppose you copy a figure on a copier using the given scale factor. Find the scale factor from the original figure to the copy in decimal form.

  a. 200%   b. 50%

  c. 150%   d. 125%

  e. 75%   f. 25%

34. Write each fraction as a decimal and as a percent.

  a. $\frac{2}{5}$ b. $\frac{3}{4}$

  c. $\frac{3}{10}$ d. $\frac{1}{4}$

  e. $\frac{7}{10}$ f. $\frac{7}{20}$

  g. $\frac{4}{5}$ h. $\frac{7}{8}$

  i. $\frac{15}{20}$ j. $\frac{3}{5}$

35. For parts (a)–(d), tell whether the figures are mathematically similar. Explain your reasoning. If the figures are similar, give the scale factor from the left figure to the right figure.

a.

b.

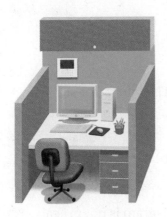 

c.

d.

For Exercises 36–38, decide whether the statement is true or false. Explain your reasoning.

36. All squares are similar.

37. All rectangles are similar.

38. If the scale factor between two similar shapes is 1, then the two shapes are the same size.

39. a. Suppose the following rectangle is reduced by a scale factor of 50%. What are the dimensions of the reduced rectangle?

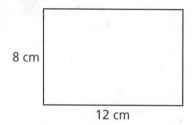

8 cm

12 cm

b. Suppose the reduced rectangle from part (a) is reduced again by a scale factor of 50%. What are the dimensions of the new rectangle? Explain your reasoning.

c. How does the reduced rectangle from part (b) compare to the original rectangle from part (a)?

40. Multiple Choice What is the value of x? The diagram is not to scale.

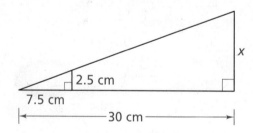

2.5 cm

7.5 cm

30 cm

x

A. 3 cm

B. 10 cm

C. 12 cm

D. 90 cm

For Exercises 41 and 42, find the missing side length. The diagrams are not to scale.

41.

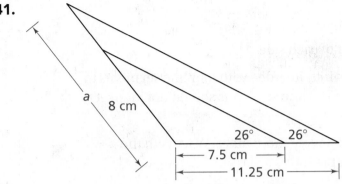

42.

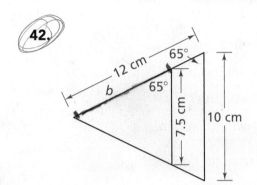

Extensions

43. Trace each shape. Divide each shape into four smaller, identical pieces that are similar to the original shape.

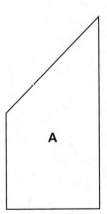

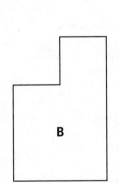

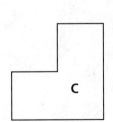

44. The **midpoint** of a line segment is a point that divides the segment into two segments of equal length. Draw a figure on grid paper by following these steps:

Step 1: Draw a large square.

Step 2: Mark the midpoint of each side.

Step 3: Connect the midpoints, in order, with four line segments to form a new figure. (The line segments should not intersect inside the square.)

Step 4: Repeat Steps 2 and 3 three more times. Work with the newest figure each time.

a. What kind of figure is formed when the midpoints of the sides of a square are connected?

b. Find the area of the original square you drew in Step 1.

c. Find the area of each of the new figures that was formed.

d. How do the areas change between successive figures?

e. Are there any similar figures in your final drawing? Explain.

45. Repeat Exercise 44 starting with an equilateral triangle, connecting three line segments to form a new triangle each time.

46. Suppose Rectangle A is similar to Rectangle B and to Rectangle C. Can you conclude that Rectangle B is similar to Rectangle C? Explain. Use drawings and examples to illustrate your answer.

47. You can subdivide figures to get smaller figures that are mathematically similar to the original. The mathematician Benoit Mandelbrot called these figures *fractals*. A famous example is the Sierpinski triangle.

Sierpinski Triangle

You can follow these steps to make the Sierpinski triangle.

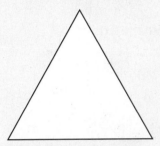

Step 1: Draw a triangle. (It does not have to be an equilateral triangle.)

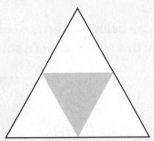

Step 2: Mark the midpoint of each side. Connect the midpoints to form four identical triangles that are similar to the original. Shade the center triangle.

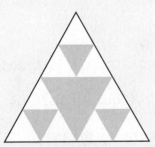

Step 3: For each unshaded triangle, mark the midpoints. Connect them in order to form four identical triangles. Shade the center triangle in each case.

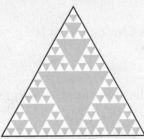

Step 4: Repeat Steps 2 and 3 over and over. To make a real Sierpinski triangle, you need to repeat the process an infinite number of times! This triangle shows five subdivisions.

a. Follow the steps for making the Sierpinski triangle until you subdivide the original triangle three times.

b. Describe any patterns you observe in your figure.

c. Mandelbrot used the term *self-similar* to describe fractals like the Sierpinski triangle. What do you think this term means?

Use the paragraph below for Exercises 48–52.

When you find the area of a square, you multiply the length of one side by itself. For a square with a side length of 3 units, you multiply 3×3 to get 9 square units. For this reason, mathematicians call 9 the *square* of 3.

The *square root* of 9 is 3. The symbol $\sqrt{}$ is used for the square root. This gives the fact family below.

$$3^2 = 9$$
$$\sqrt{9} = 3$$

48. The square below has an area of 10 square units. Write the side length of this square using a square root symbol.

49. Multiple Choice What is the square root of 144?

    F. 7   **G.** 12   **H.** 72   **J.** 20,736

50. What is the side length of a square with an area of 144 square units?

51. You have learned that if a figure grows by a scale factor of s, the area of the figure grows by a factor of s^2. If the area of a figure grows by a factor of f, what is the scale factor?

52. Find three examples of squares and square roots in the work you have done so far in this Unit.

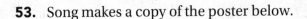

53. Song makes a copy of the poster below.

12 in.

9 in.

a. She presses the 50% button on the copy machine. Now the length and width of the poster are each half of their original sizes. Song thinks that if she enlarges the copy by 150%, the new copy will be the same size as the original. Is she correct?

b. Suppose Song had done the opposite in part (a), first enlarging the poster by 150%, and then reducing the copy by 50%. Will the final copy be the same size as the original? Will it be the same size as the copy made in part (a)?

c. Song uses the same process from parts (a) and (b) with a different-sized poster. Does she get similar results?

d. Song applied a scale factor of 25% to shrink the original poster. Now she wants to get the poster back to the original size. What scale factor should she use? Explain your reasoning.

e. Suppose Song had used 75% and 125% in parts (a) and (b) instead of 50% and 150%. What would have happened?

f. What general statements can you make about applying any pair of two scale factors one after the other? Consider a pair of two enlargements, a pair of two reductions, and a pair consisting of one enlargement and one reduction.

In this Investigation, you explored similar polygons and scale factors. The following questions will help you summarize what you have learned.

Think about these questions. Discuss your ideas with other students and your teacher. Then write a summary of your findings in your notebook.

1. **a.** If two polygons are similar, **how** can you find the scale factor from one polygon to the other? Give specific examples.

   b. Suppose you are given a polygon. **How** can you draw a similar figure?

2. **What** does the scale factor between two similar figures tell you about the

   a. side lengths?

   b. perimeters?

   c. areas?

   d. angles?

3. If two figures are similar, **how** can you find a missing side length?

4. **Describe** how you can find the measure of a distance that you cannot measure directly.

5. **What** does it mean to say two shapes are similar? After completing Investigation 3, how can you build on your statements from Mathematical Reflections 1 and 2?

   "Two geometric shapes are similar when . . ."

Common Core Mathematical Practices

As you worked on the Problems in this Investigation, you used prior knowledge to make sense of them. You also applied Mathematical Practices to solve the Problems. Think back over your work, the ways you thought about the Problems, and how you used Mathematical Practices.

Elena described her thoughts in the following way:

We were trying to solve a realistic problem in Problem 3.4. We needed to find the distance across a river.

We looked at a diagram where some distances and angles were labeled. The diagram included similar triangles. We used properties of similar triangles to help us find the distance across the river. We presented our work to the class.

Matt wondered how we knew which sides were corresponding. We used the picture to explain which sides were corresponding and why.

....

Common Core Standards for Mathematical Practice
MP4 Model with mathematics

- What other Mathematical Practices can you identify in Elena's reasoning?

- Describe a Mathematical Practice that you and your classmates used to solve a different Problem in this Investigation.

Investigation 4

Similarity and Ratios

You can enhance a report or story by adding photographs, drawings, or diagrams. If you place a graphic in an electronic document, you can enlarge, reduce, or move it. When you click on the graphic, it appears inside a frame with handles along the sides, such as the figure shown below.

You can change the size and shape of the image by dragging the handles.

Common Core State Standards

7.RP.A.2 Recognize and represent proportional relationships between quantities.

7.RP.A.3 Use proportional relationships to solve multistep ratio and percent problems.

7.EE.B.4 Use variables to represent quantities in a real-world or mathematical problem, and construct simple equations and inequalities to solve problems by reasoning about the quantities.

7.G.A.1 Solve problems involving scale drawings of geometric figures, including computing actual lengths and areas from a scale drawing and reproducing a scale drawing at a different scale.

Also 7.G.B.6, 7.RP.A.2a, 7.RP.A.2b, 7.EE.B.3, and 7.EE.B.4a

Here are examples of the image after it has been resized.

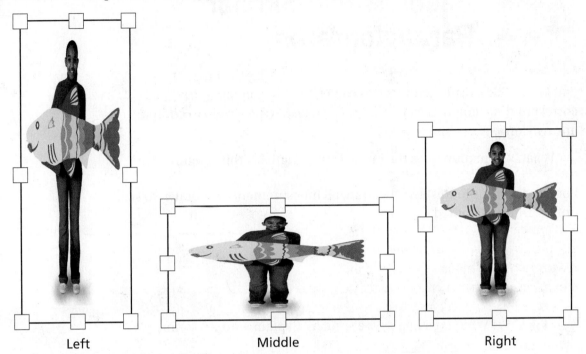

Left   Middle   Right

- How did this technique produce these variations of the original shape?
- Which of these images appears to be similar to the original? Why?

You can use ratios to describe and compare shapes. A **ratio** is a comparison of two quantities, such as two lengths. The rectangle around the original figure is about 10 centimeters tall and 8 centimeters wide. You can say, "The ratio of height to width is 10 to 8."

This table gives the ratios of height to width for the images.

Image Information

Figure	Height (cm)	Width (cm)	Height-to-Width Ratio
Original	10	8	10 to 8
Left	8	3	8 to 3
Middle	3	6	3 to 6
Right	5	4	5 to 4

- What do you notice about the height-to-width ratios?

The comparisons "10 to 8" and "5 to 4" are *equivalent ratios*. **Equivalent ratios** are like equivalent fractions. In fact, ratios are often written in fraction form. You can express equivalent ratios with equations. A **proportion** is an equation stating that two ratios are equal.

$$\frac{10}{8} = \frac{5}{4} \qquad \frac{8}{10} = \frac{4}{5}$$

4.1 Ratios Within Similar Parallelograms

You know that a scale factor relates each length in a figure to the corresponding length in its image. You can also write a ratio to compare any two lengths in a single figure.

- What information does the ratio of side lengths within a figure give?

For the diagrams in this Investigation, all measurements are drawn to scale unless otherwise noted.

Problem 4.1

Ⓐ 1. Which rectangles are similar? Explain your reasoning.

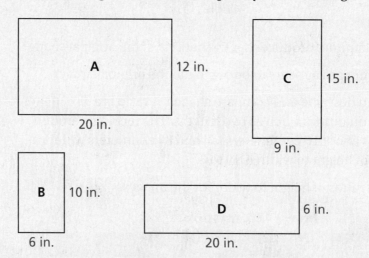

2. a. For each rectangle, find the ratio of the length of a short side to the length of a long side.

b. What do you notice about the ratios in part (a) for similar rectangles? About the ratios for non-similar rectangles?

3. Choose two similar rectangles. Find the scale factor from the smaller rectangle to the larger rectangle. What does the scale factor tell you?

4. Compare the information given by the scale factor from part (3) to the information given by the ratios of side lengths from part (2).

Problem 4.1 *continued*

B 1. Which of the parallelograms below are similar? Explain.

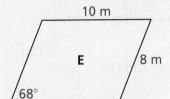

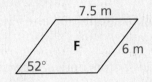

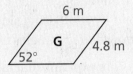

2. For each parallelogram, find the ratio of the length of a long side to the length of a short side. How do the ratios compare?

C 1. Suppose you find the ratio of the lengths of **adjacent sides,** two sides that meet at a vertex, in a rectangle. This ratio is equivalent to the ratio of the corresponding side lengths in another rectangle. Are the figures similar? Explain your reasoning.

2. Suppose you find the ratio of the lengths of adjacent sides in a parallelogram. This ratio is equivalent to the ratio of the adjacent sides in another parallelogram. Are the figures similar? Explain.

A C E Homework starts on page 90.

Did You Know?

Hancock Place is an office building in Boston, Massachusetts. The tower of the building has a unique shape. While most office buildings are rectangular, the base of the tower of Hancock Place is a parallelogram. This makes the tower look two-dimensional from some vantage points.

4.2 Ratios Within Similar Triangles

Since all rectangles have four 90° angles, you can show that rectangles are similar by comparing side lengths. Jounique and Curtis each have methods to show that rectangles are similar.

Jounique explains that all scale factors between corresponding side lengths are equal for similar rectangles.

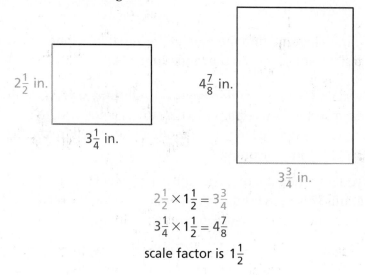

$$2\tfrac{1}{2} \times 1\tfrac{1}{2} = 3\tfrac{3}{4}$$
$$3\tfrac{1}{4} \times 1\tfrac{1}{2} = 4\tfrac{7}{8}$$
scale factor is $1\tfrac{1}{2}$

Curtis says that rectangles are similar if the ratios of corresponding adjacent sides within each shape are proportional.

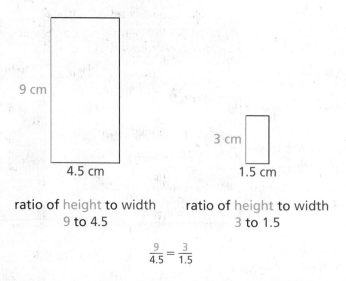

ratio of height to width   ratio of height to width
     9 to 4.5   3 to 1.5

$$\frac{9}{4.5} = \frac{3}{1.5}$$

You need to compare more than just side lengths of polygons to understand their shapes. In this Problem, you will use angle measures and side-length ratios to find similar triangles.

Problem 4.2

For Questions A and B, use the triangles below. The triangles are drawn to scale.

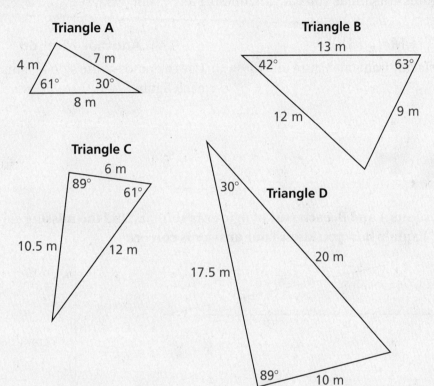

A Which triangles are similar? Explain your reasoning.

B **1.** Within each triangle, find the ratio of shortest side to longest side. Find the ratio of shortest side to "middle" side.

2. What do you notice about the ratios in part (1) for similar triangles? About the ratios for non-similar triangles?

C Choose two similar triangles. Find the scale factor from the smaller triangle to the larger triangle. What information does the scale factor give?

D Compare the information given by the ratios of side lengths in Question B to the information given by the scale factor in Question C.

A C E Homework starts on page 90.

4.3 Finding Missing Parts
Using Similarity to Find Measurements

When two figures are similar, you can find missing lengths in two ways.

One Method

Use the scale factor from one figure to the other.

 OR

Another Method

Use the ratios of the side lengths within each figure.

 Problem 4.3

For Questions A and B, each pair of figures is similar. Find the missing side lengths. Explain how you know your answer is correct.

A

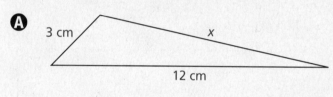

3 cm   *x*

12 cm

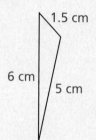

1.5 cm

6 cm

5 cm

B

x

1.5 cm

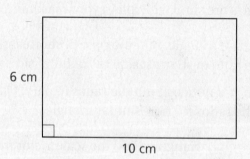

6 cm

10 cm

Problem 4.3 *continued*

C The parallelograms below are similar. Find the missing measurements. Explain how you found your answers.

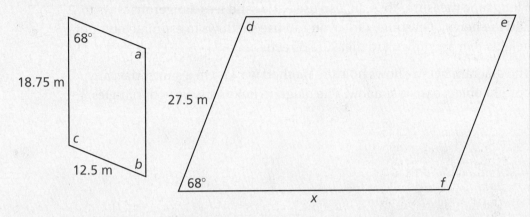

D The figures below are similar. Each side length is in centimeters.

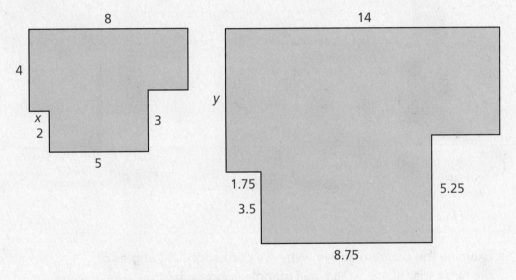

1. Find the value of *x*. Explain how you found it.

2. Find the value of *y*. Explain.

3. Find the area and perimeter of one of the figures.

4. Use your answer to part (3) and the scale factor. Find the area and perimeter of the other figure. Explain.

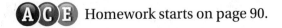 **A C E** Homework starts on page 90.

4.4 Using Shadows to Find Heights
Using Similar Triangles

 You can find the height of a school building by climbing a ladder and using a long tape measure. You can also use easier and less dangerous ways to find the height. On sunny days, you can use shadows to estimate outdoor heights that are difficult to measure directly.

The diagram below shows how the method works. On a sunny day, any upright object casts a shadow. The diagram below shows two triangles.

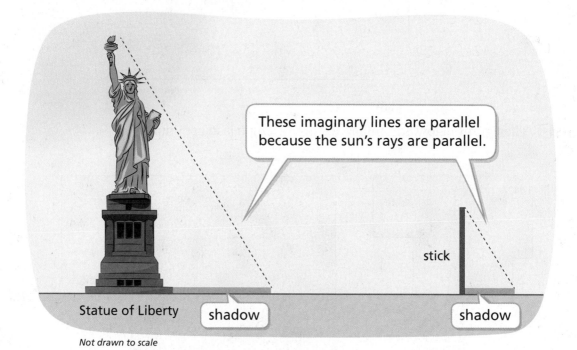

These imaginary lines are parallel because the sun's rays are parallel.

stick

Statue of Liberty   shadow   shadow

Not drawn to scale

- Examine the diagram above. Why are corresponding angles of the large triangle and the small triangle congruent?
- What does this suggest about the similarity of the triangles?
- How can you use the shadows to find the height of the Statue of Liberty?

To use the shadow method, measure the following:

- the length of the stick
- the length of the stick's shadow
- the length of the building's shadow

Problem 4.4

Your teacher will assign you an object such as a flagpole, clock tower, or school. Use the shadow method to find the height of the object.

A Make the necessary measurements. Sketch a diagram and record your measurements on the sketch.

B Use similar triangles and your sketch to find the height of the object.

C When you use the shadow method, what problems might affect the accuracy of your answer? Explain.

D A tree casts a 25-foot shadow. At the same time, a 6-foot stick casts a shadow 4.5 feet long. How tall is the tree?

A C E Homework starts on page 90.

The Statue of Liberty is about 111 feet tall from head to toe. When she casts a 600-foot-long shadow, her head casts a shadow about 93½ feet long. You can use that information to find the height of her head.

Applications

1. For parts (a)–(c), use the parallelograms below.

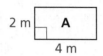

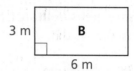

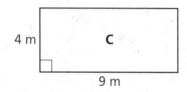

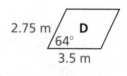

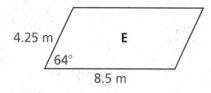

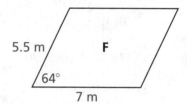

a. List all the pairs of similar parallelograms. Explain your reasoning.

b. For each pair of similar parallelograms, find the ratio of two adjacent side lengths in one parallelogram. Find the ratio of the corresponding side lengths in the other parallelogram. How do these ratios compare?

c. For each pair of similar parallelograms, find the scale factor from one shape to the other. Explain how the information given by the scale factors is different from the information given by the ratios of adjacent side lengths.

2. a. On grid paper, draw two similar rectangles where the scale factor from one rectangle to the other is 2.5. Label the length and width of each rectangle.

b. For each rectangle, find the ratio of the length to the width.

c. Draw a third rectangle that is similar to one of the rectangles in part (a). Find the scale factor from the new rectangle to the one from part (a).

d. Find the ratio of the length to the width for the new rectangle.

e. What can you say about the length-to-width ratios of the three rectangles? Is this true for another rectangle that is similar to one of the three rectangles? Explain.

3. For parts (a)–(d), use the triangles below. The drawings are not to scale.

Triangle A

6.5 in.

25°

3 in.   136°   4 in.

Triangle B

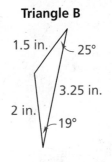

1.5 in.   25°

3.25 in.

2 in.

19°

Triangle C

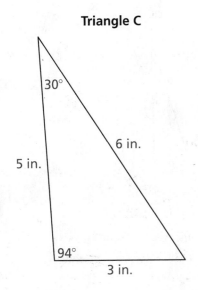

30°

6 in.

5 in.

94°

3 in.

Triangle D

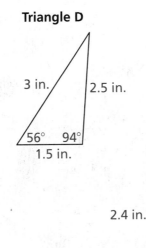

3 in.   2.5 in.

56°   94°

1.5 in.

Triangle E

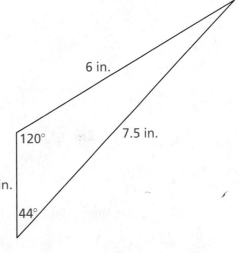

6 in.

120°   7.5 in.

2.4 in.

44°

a. List all the pairs of similar triangles. Explain why they are similar.

b. For each pair of similar triangles, find the ratio of two side lengths in one triangle. Find the ratio of the corresponding side lengths in the other. How do these ratios compare?

c. For each pair of similar triangles, find the scale factor from one shape to the other. Explain how the information given by the scale factors is different than the information given by the ratios of side lengths.

d. How are corresponding angles related in similar triangles? Is it the same relationship as for corresponding side lengths? Explain.

For Exercises 4–7, each pair of figures is similar. Find the missing measurement. Explain your reasoning. (Note: The figures are not drawn to scale.)

4.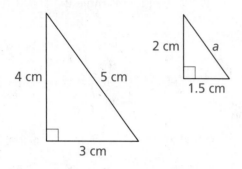

5.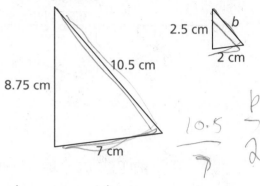

6.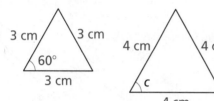

7.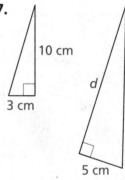

For Exercises 8–10, Rectangles A and B are similar.

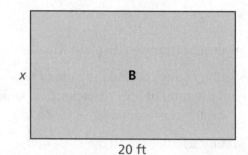

8. **Multiple Choice** What is the value of *x*?

    A. 4   **B.** 12   **C.** 15   **D.** $33\frac{1}{3}$

9. What is the scale factor from Rectangle B to Rectangle A?

10. Find the area of each rectangle. How are the areas related?

11. Rectangles C and D are similar.

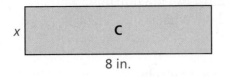

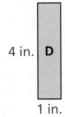

a. What is the value of x?

b. What is the scale factor from Rectangle C to Rectangle D?

c. Find the area of each rectangle. How are the areas related?

12. Suppose you want to buy new carpeting for your bedroom. The bedroom floor is a 9-foot-by-12-foot rectangle. Carpeting is sold by the square yard.

a. How much carpeting do you need to buy?

b. Carpeting costs $22 per square yard. How much will the carpet cost?

13. Suppose you want to buy the carpet described in Exercise 12 for a library. The library floor is similar to the floor of the 9-foot-by-12-foot bedroom. The scale factor from the bedroom to the library is 2.5.

a. What are the dimensions of the library? Explain.

b. How much carpeting do you need for the library?

c. How much will the carpet for the library cost?

14. The Washington Monument is the tallest structure in Washington, D.C. At a certain time, the monument casts a shadow that is about 500 feet long. At the same time, a 40-foot flagpole nearby casts a shadow that is about 36 feet long. About how tall is the monument? Sketch a diagram.

15. Darius uses the shadow method to estimate the height of a flagpole. He finds that a 5-foot stick casts a 4-foot shadow. At the same time, he finds that the flagpole casts a 20-foot shadow. What is the height of the flagpole? Sketch a diagram.

16. a. Greg and Zola are trying to find the height of their school building. Zola takes a picture of Greg standing next to the building. How might this picture help them determine the height of the building?

b. Greg is 5 feet tall. The picture Zola took shows Greg as $\frac{1}{4}$ inch tall. If the building is 25 feet tall in real life, how tall should the building be in the picture? Explain.

c. In part (a), you thought of ways to use a picture to find the height of an object. Think of an object in your school that is difficult to measure directly, such as a high wall, bookshelf, or trophy case. Describe how you might find the height of the object.

17. Movie screens often have an *aspect ratio* of 16 by 9. This means that for every 16 feet of width along the base of the screen there are 9 feet of height. The width of the screen at a local drive-in theater is about 115 feet wide. The screen has a 16 : 9 aspect ratio. About how tall is the screen?

18. Triangle A has sides that measure 4 inches, 5 inches, and 6 inches. Triangle B has sides that measure 8 feet, 10 feet, and 12 feet. Taylor and Landon are discussing whether the two triangles are similar. Do you agree with Taylor or with Landon? Explain.

Taylor's Explanation

The triangles are similar. If you double each of the side lengths of Triangle A, you get the side lengths for Triangle B.

Landon's Explanation

The triangles are not similar. Taylor's method works when the two measures have the same units. However, the sides of Triangle A are measured in inches, and the sides of Triangle B are measured in feet. So, they cannot be similar.

Connections

For Exercises 19–24, tell whether each pair of ratios is equivalent.

19. 3 to 2 and 5 to 4

20. 8 to 4 and 12 to 8

21. 7 to 5 and 21 to 15

22. 1.5 to 0.5 and 6 to 2

23. 1 to 2 and 3.5 to 6

24. 2 to 3 and 4 to 6

25. Use a pair of equivalent ratios from Exercises 19–24. Write a similarity problem using the ratios. Explain how to solve the problem.

For each ratio in Exercises 26–29, write two other equivalent ratios.

26. 5 to 3

27. 4 to 1

28. 3 to 7

29. 1.5 to 1

30. Here is a picture of Duke. The scale factor from Duke to the picture is 12.5%. Use an inch ruler to make any measurements.

a. How long is Duke from his nose to the tip of his tail? Explain how you used the picture to find your answer.

b. To build a doghouse for Duke, you need to know his height. How tall is Duke? Explain.

c. A copy center has a machine that prints on poster-size paper. You can resize an image from 50% to 200%. How can you use the machine to make a life-size picture of Duke?

31. Paloma draws triangle *ABC* on a grid. She applies a rule to make the triangle on the right.

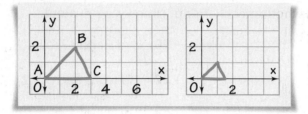

    a. What rule did Paloma apply to make the new triangle?

    b. Is the new triangle similar to triangle *ABC*? Explain your reasoning. If the triangles are similar, give the scale factor from triangle *ABC* to the new triangle.

For Exercises 32 and 33, use the paragraph below.

The Rosavilla School District wants to build a new middle school building. They ask architects to make scale drawings of possible layouts for the building. Two possibilities are shown below.

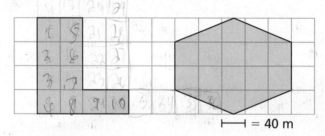

$\vdash\!\!-\!\!\dashv = 40$ m

32. a. What is the area of each scale drawing in square units?

    b. What would the area of the ground floor of each building be?

33. **Multiple Choice** The school board likes the L-shaped layout but wants a building with more space. They increase the L-shaped layout by a scale factor of 2. For the new layout, choose the correct statement.

    F. The area is two times the original.

    G. The area is four times the original.

    H. The area is eight times the original.

    J. None of the statements above are correct.

34. The school principal visits Ashton's class one day. Ashton uses the mirror method to estimate the principal's height. This diagram shows the measurements he records.

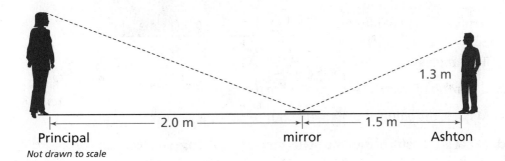

Principal   2.0 m   mirror   1.5 m   Ashton   1.3 m

Not drawn to scale

a. What estimate should Ashton give for the principal's height?

b. Is your answer to part (a) a reasonable height for an adult?

35. Use the table for parts (a)–(c).

Student Heights and Arm Spans

Height (in.)	60	65	63	50	58	66	60	63	67	65
Arm Span (in.)	55	60	60	48	60	65	60	67	62	70

a. Find the ratio of arm span to height for each student. Write the ratio as a fraction. Then write the ratio as an equivalent decimal. What patterns do you notice?

b. Find the mean of the ratios.

c. Use your answer from part (b). Predict the arm span of a person who is 62 inches tall. Explain your reasoning.

36. For each angle measure, find the measure of its complement and the measure of its supplement.

Sample: $30°$ complement: $60°$; supplement: $150°$

a. $20°$ **b.** $70°$ **c.** $45°$

37. The rectangles at the right are similar.

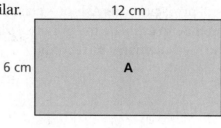

12 cm

x

6 cm

A

4 cm   B

a. What is the scale factor from Rectangle A to Rectangle B?

b. Complete the following sentence in two different ways. Use the side lengths of Rectangles A and B.

  The ratio of ▪ *to* ▪ *is equivalent to the ratio of* ▪ *to* ▪.

c. What is the value of *x*? Explain your reasoning.

d. What is the ratio of the area of Rectangle A to the area of Rectangle B?

For Exercises 38 and 39, use the rectangles below.

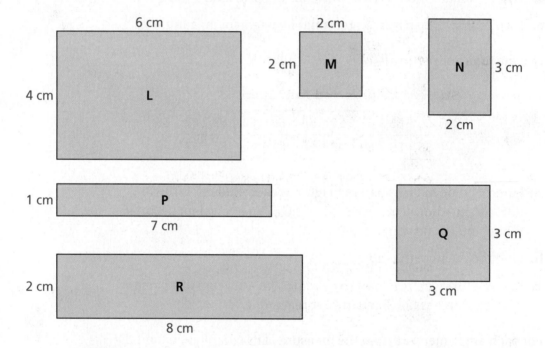

6 cm

2 cm

4 cm   L

2 cm   M

N   3 cm

2 cm

1 cm   P

7 cm

Q   3 cm

2 cm   R

3 cm

8 cm

38. Multiple Choice Which pair of rectangles listed below is similar?

  A. L and M   **B.** L and Q   **C.** L and N   **D.** P and R

39. a. Find at least one more pair of similar rectangles.

  b. For each pair of similar rectangles, find the scale factor from the larger rectangle to the smaller rectangle. Find the scale factor from the smaller rectangle to the larger rectangle.

  c. For each similar pair of rectangles, find the ratio of the area of the larger rectangle to the area of the smaller rectangle.

Extensions

40. For parts (a)–(e), use the similar triangles below.

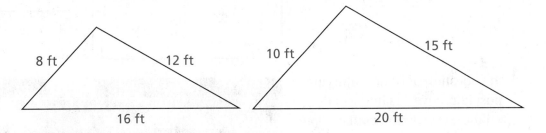

 a. What is the scale factor from the smaller triangle to the larger triangle? Write your answer as a fraction and a decimal.

 b. Choose any side of the larger triangle. Find the ratio of this side length to the corresponding side length in the smaller triangle. Write your answer as a fraction and as a decimal. How does the ratio compare to the scale factor from part (a)?

 c. What is the scale factor from the larger triangle to the smaller triangle? Write your answer as a fraction and a decimal.

 d. Choose any side of the smaller triangle. Find the ratio of this side length to the corresponding side length in the larger triangle. Write your answer as a fraction and as a decimal. How does the ratio compare to the scale factor from part (c)?

 e. What patterns do you notice in parts (a)–(d)? Are these patterns the same for any pair of similar figures? Explain.

41. For parts (a) and (b), use a straightedge and an angle ruler or protractor.

 a. Draw two different triangles that each have angle measures of 30°, 60°, and 90°. Do the triangles appear to be similar?

 b. Draw two different triangles that each have angle measures of 40°, 80°, and 60°. Do the triangles appear to be similar?

 c. Based on your findings for parts (a) and (b), make a conjecture about triangles with congruent angle measures.

42. One of these rectangles is "most pleasing to the eye."

A

B

C

The question of what shapes are most attractive has interested builders, artists, and craftspeople for thousands of years.

The ancient Greeks were particularly attracted to rectangular shapes similar to Rectangle B above. They referred to such shapes as "golden rectangles." They used golden rectangles frequently in buildings and monuments. The ratio of the length to the width in a golden rectangle is called the "golden ratio."

This photograph of the Parthenon (a temple in Athens, Greece) shows several golden rectangles.

a. Measure the length and width of Rectangles A, B, and C above in centimeters. For each rectangle, estimate the ratio of the length to the width as accurately as possible. The ratio for Rectangle B is an approximation of the golden ratio.

b. You can divide a golden rectangle into a square and a smaller rectangle similar to the original rectangle.

Golden Rectangle

The smaller rectangle is similar to the larger rectangle.

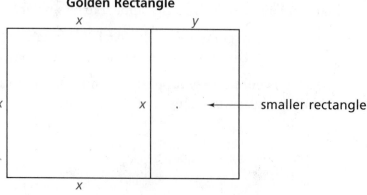

smaller rectangle

Copy Rectangle B above. Divide this golden rectangle into a square and a rectangle. Is the smaller rectangle a golden rectangle? Explain.

43. For parts (a) and (b), use the triangles below.

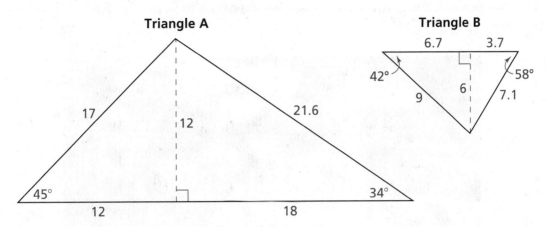

Triangle A

Triangle B

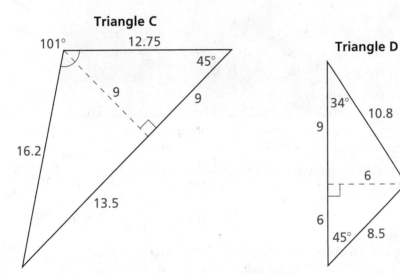

Triangle C

Triangle D

a. Identify the triangles that are similar to each other. Explain your reasoning.

b. For each triangle, find the ratio of the base to the height. How do these ratios compare for the similar triangles? How do these ratios compare for the non-similar triangles?

For Exercises 44–48, suppose a photographer for the school newspaper took this picture. The editors want to resize the photo to fit in a specific space on a page.

4 in.

6 in.

44. Can the original photo be changed to a similar rectangle with the given measurements (in inches)?

    a. 8 by 12   **b.** 9 by 11   **c.** 6 by 9   **d.** 3 by 4.5

45. Suppose that the school copier only has three paper sizes (in inches): $8\frac{1}{2}$ by 11, 11 by 14, and 11 by 17. You can enlarge or reduce documents by specifying a percent from 50% to 200%. Can you make copies of the photo that fit exactly on any of the three paper sizes? Explain your reasoning.

46. A copy machine accepts scale factors from 50% to 200%. How can you use the copy machine to produce a copy that is 25% of the original photo's size? How does the area of the copy relate to the area of the original photo?

47. How can you use the copy machine to reduce the photo to a copy that is 12.5% of the original photo's size? 36% of the original photo's size? How does the area of the reduced figure compare to the area of the original in each case?

48. What is the greatest enlargement of the photo that will fit on paper that is 11 inches by 17 inches?

49. The following sequence of numbers is called the *Fibonacci sequence*. It is named after an Italian mathematician from the 14th century who contributed to the early development of algebra.

$$1, 1, 2, 3, 5, 8, 13, 21, 34, 55, 89, 144, 233, 377 \ldots$$

a. Look for patterns in this sequence. How are the numbers found? Use your ideas to find the next four terms.

b. Find the ratio of each term to the term before it. For example, 1 to 1, 2 to 1, 3 to 2, and so on. Write each of the ratios as a fraction and as an equivalent decimal. Compare the results to the golden ratios you found in Exercise 44. Describe similarities and differences.

50. Francisco, Katya, and Peter notice that all squares are similar. They wonder if other shapes that have four sides are *all-similar*. Who is correct?

Francisco's Work

Squares are the only type of *all-similar* polygon with four sides. This is because all the sides have equal length, and all the angles are right angles.

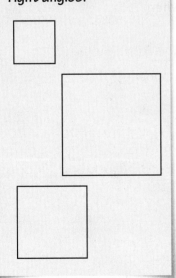

Katya's Work

All rectangles are *all-similar*. Just like squares, all the angles in rectangles are congruent.

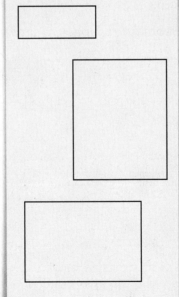

Peter's Work

I know that rhombi are four-sided shapes with sides that are all the same length. Rhombi must be *all-similar* because, for two rhombi, there is a consistent scale factor for all corresponding side lengths.

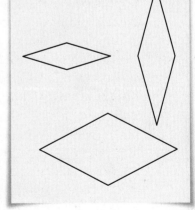

51. Ernie and Vernon are having a discussion about *all-similar* shapes. Ernie says that regular polygons and circles are the only types of *all-similar* shapes. Vernon claims isosceles right triangles are *all-similar,* but they are not regular polygons. Who is correct? Explain.

Mathematical Reflections

In this Investigation, you used ratios to describe and compare the size and shape of rectangles, triangles, and other figures. The following questions will help you summarize what you have learned.

Think about these questions. Discuss your ideas with other students and your teacher. Then write a summary of your findings in your notebook.

1. If two triangles, rectangles, or parallelograms are similar,

   a. **How** does the ratio of two side lengths within one figure compare to the ratio of the corresponding side lengths in the other figure?

   b. **What** does the scale factor from one figure to the other tell you about the figures?

2. a. **Describe** at least two ways to find a missing side length in a pair of similar figures.

   b. **How** can you find the height of an object that cannot be measured directly?

3. **What** does it mean to say that two shapes are similar? After exploring with ratios, build on your statements from Mathematical Reflections 1, 2, and 3:

   "Two geometric shapes are similar when. . ."

Common Core Mathematical Practices

As you worked on the Problems in this Investigation, you used prior knowledge to make sense of them. You also applied Mathematical Practices to solve the Problems. Think back over your work, the ways you thought about the Problems, and how you used Mathematical Practices.

Shawna described her thoughts in the following way:

We looked at two similar rectangles in Problem 4.1. For each rectangle, we determined the ratio of length to width. We noticed that the ratios were equal. This was not true for two non-similar rectangles.

We also looked at the ratio of a side length in one rectangle to the corresponding side length in a similar rectangle. This ratio always gave us the scale factor between the two rectangles. This makes sense since you multiply each side length of one rectangle by the scale factor to find the corresponding side length in the similar rectangle.

We noticed that these patterns are true for parallelograms and triangles, too.

Common Core Standards for Mathematical Practice

MP2 Reason abstractly and quantitatively

- What other Mathematical Practices can you identify in Shawna's reasoning?

- Describe a Mathematical Practice that you and your classmates used to solve a different Problem in this Investigation.

Unit Project

Shrinking or Enlarging Pictures

Your final project for this Unit involves two parts:

1. the drawing of a similar image of a picture
2. a written report on making similar figures

Part 1: Drawing

You will enlarge or shrink a picture or cartoon of your choice. Be sure to choose a picture that has lengths, angles, and areas that you will be able to measure and compare. You will use coordinate graphing rules to produce a similar image.

If you enlarge the picture, the image must have a scale factor of at least 4.

If you shrink the picture, the image must have a scale factor of at most $\frac{1}{4}$.

Your final project must be presented in a display for others. Both the original picture and the image need to be in the display, and you must do the following:

- identify the scale factor and show how the lengths compare between the picture and the image;

- identify two pairs of corresponding angles and show how the angles compare between the picture and the image;

- compare some area of the picture with the corresponding area of the image.

Part 2: Write a Report

Write a report describing how you made your similar figure. Your report should include the following:

- a description of the technique or method you used to make the image;

- a description of changes in the lengths, angles, and area between the original picture and the image;

- a paragraph (or more) on other details that you think are interesting or that help the reader understand what they see (for example, a description of any problems or challenges you had and decisions you made as a result).

The Problems in this Unit helped you understand the concept of similarity as it applies to geometric shapes. You learned how to

- make similar shapes or scale drawings

- determine whether or not two shapes are similar

- relate side lengths, perimeters, angle measures, and areas of similar shapes to each other

- use similarity to solve problems

Use Your Understanding: Similarity

Test your understanding of similarity by solving the following problems.

1. The square below is subdivided into triangles and parallelograms. Some of the shapes are similar.

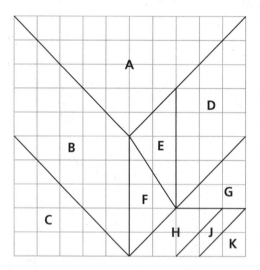

a. List all the pairs of similar triangles in the figure. For each pair, give the scale factor from one figure to the other.

b. Pick a pair of similar triangles. Explain how their perimeters are related and how their areas are related.

c. List several pairs of triangles in the figure that are *not* similar.

d. List all pairs of similar parallelograms in the figure. For each pair, give the scale factor from one figure to the other.

e. Pick a pair of similar parallelograms. Explain how their perimeters are related and how their areas are related.

f. List several pairs of parallelograms in the figure that are *not* similar.

2. **a.** Suppose a triangle is drawn on a coordinate grid. Which of the following rules will change the triangle into a similar triangle?

   i. $(3x, 3y)$ **ii.** $(x + 3, y + 2)$

  iii. $(2x, 4y)$ **iv.** $(2x, 2y + 1)$

   v. $(1.5x, 1.5y)$ **vi.** $(x - 3, 2y - 3)$

b. For each of the rules in part (a) that will produce a similar triangle, give the scale factor from the original triangle to its image.

3. A photo of the after-school pottery class measures 12 centimeters by 20 centimeters. The class officers want to enlarge the photo to fit on a large poster.

a. Can the original photo be enlarged to 60 centimeters by 90 centimeters?

b. Can the original photo be enlarged to 42 centimeters by 70 centimeters?

12 cm

20 cm

Explain Your Reasoning

Answer the following questions to summarize what you know.

4. What questions do you ask yourself when deciding whether two shapes are similar?

5. Suppose Shape A is similar to Shape B. The scale factor from Shape A to Shape B is k.

   a. How are the perimeters of the two figures related?

   b. How are the areas of the two figures related?

6. If two triangles are similar, what do you know about the following measurements?

   a. the side lengths of the two figures

   b. the angle measures of the two figures

7. Tell whether each statement is true or false. Explain.

   a. Any two equilateral triangles are similar.

   b. Any two rectangles are similar.

   c. Any two squares are similar.

   d. Any two isosceles triangles are similar.

English / Spanish Glossary

A   **adjacent sides**   Two sides that meet at a vertex. In this rectangle, sides *AB* and *AD* are adjacent because they meet at vertex A.

lados adyacentes   Son dos lados que coinciden en un vértice. En este rectángulo, los lados *AB* y *AD* son adyacentes porque coinciden en el vértice *A*.

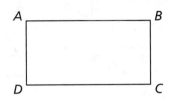

C   **compare**   Academic Vocabulary   To tell or show how two things are alike and different.

related terms   *analyze, relate, resemble*

sample: Compare the ratios of each of the corresponding side lengths for the similar triangles shown below.

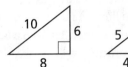

> The ratios of the corresponding side lengths of two triangles are $\frac{3}{6}$, $\frac{4}{8}$, and $\frac{5}{10}$. Each of these ratios equals $\frac{1}{2}$, so all of the ratios of the corresponding side lengths are equal.

comparar   Vocabulario académico   Decir o mostrar en qué se parecen y en qué se diferencian dos cosas.

términos relacionados   *analizar, relacionar, parecerse*

ejemplo: Compara las razones de las longitudes de lado correspondientes para los triángulos que se muestran.

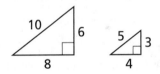

> Las razones de las langitudes de lado correspondientes de dos triángulos son $\frac{3}{6}$, $\frac{4}{8}$ y $\frac{5}{10}$. Cada una de estas razones es igual a $\frac{1}{2}$, por lo tanto todas las razones de las longitudes de lado correspondientes son iguales.

corresponding angles Corresponding angles have the same relative position in similar figures. In this pair of similar shapes, angle *BCD* corresponds to angle *JKF*.

ángulos correspondientes Los ángulos correspondientes tienen la misma posición relativa en figuras semejantes. En el siguiente par de figuras semejantes, el ángulo *BCD* corresponde al ángulo *JKF*.

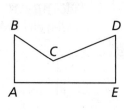 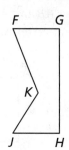

corresponding sides Corresponding sides have the same relative position in similar figures. In the pair of similar shapes above, side *AB* corresponds to side *HJ*.

lados correspondientes Los lados correspondientes tienen la misma posición relativa en figuras semejantes. En las dos figuras semejantes que se muestran abajo, el lado *AB* corresponde al lado *HJ*.

E **equivalent ratios** Ratios whose fraction representations are equivalent are called equivalent ratios. For instance, the ratios 3 to 4 and 6 to 8 are equivalent because $\frac{3}{4} = \frac{6}{8}$.

razones equivalentes Las razones cuyas representaciones de fracciones son equivalentes se llaman razones equivalentes. Por ejemplo, las razones 3 a 4 y 6 a 8 son equivalentes porque $\frac{3}{4} = \frac{6}{8}$.

estimate Academic Vocabulary To find an approximate answer that is relatively close to an exact amount.

related terms *approximate, guess*

sample: Estimate the scale factor for the similar rectangles shown below.

hacer una estimación Vocabulario académico Hallar una respuesta aproximada que esté relativamente cerca de una cantidad exacta.

términos relacionados *aproximar, suponer*

ejemplo: Estima el factor de escala para los rectángulos semejantes que se muestran.

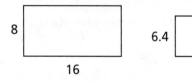

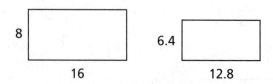

The side length 6.4 in the smaller rectangle corresponds to the side length 8 in the larger rectangle. Since 6.4 is about $\frac{3}{4}$ of 8, the scale factor is about $\frac{3}{4}$.

La longitud de lado 6.4 del rectángulo más pequeño corresponde a la longitud de lado 8 en el rectángulo más grande. Como 6.4 es aproximadamente $\frac{3}{4}$ de 8. El factor de escala es aproximadamente $\frac{3}{4}$.

explain Academic Vocabulary To give facts and details that make an idea easier to understand. Explaining can involve a written summary supported by a diagram, chart, table, or any combination of these.

related terms *describe, show, justify, tell, present*

sample: Consider the following similar rectangles. Is it possible to find the missing value *x*? Explain.

explicar Vocabulario académico Proporcionar datos y detalles que hagan que una idea sea más fácil de comprender. Explicar puede incluir un resumen escrito apoyado por un diagrama, una gráfica, una tabla o una combinación de estos.

términos relacionados *describir, mostrar, justificar, decir, presentar*

ejemplo: Observa los siguientes rectángulos semejantes. ¿Se puede hallar el valor de x? Explica tu respuesta.

Since I know the two rectangles are similar, I can find the scale factor. Once I know the scale factor, I can divide the side length of the larger rectangle that corresponds to the missing side length x by the scale factor. This will give me the value of x.
I can also find the value of x by writing a proportion using the scale factor as one of the ratios, $\frac{x}{5} = \frac{5}{15}$, and then solve for x.

Como sé que los dos rectángulos son semejantes, puedo hallar el factor de escala. Una vez que sepa el factor de escala, puedo dividir la longitud de lado del rectángulo más grande, que corresponde a la longitud de lado x, por el factor de escala. Eso me dará el valor de x.
También puedo hallar el valor de x al escribir una proporción usando el factor escala como una de las razones, $\frac{x}{5} = \frac{5}{15}$, y después resolver para x.

image The figure that results from some transformation of a figure. It is often of interest to consider what is the same and what is different about a figure and its image.

imagen La figura que resulta al realizar la transformación de una figura. A menudo es interesante tener en cuenta en qué se parecen y en qué se diferencian una figura y su imagen.

M **midpoint** A point that divides a line segment into two segments of equal length. In the figure below *M* is the midpoint of the segment *LN*.

punto medio Punto que divide un segmento de recta en dos segmentos de igual longitud. En la figura de abajo, *M* es el punto medio del segmento de recta *LN*.

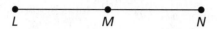

N **nested triangles** Triangles that share a common angle are sometimes called nested. In the figure below, triangle *ABC* is nested in triangle *ADE*.

triángulos semejantes Los triángulos que comparten un ángulo común a veces se llaman *semejantes*. En la siguiente figura, el triángulo *ABC* es semejante al triángulo *ADE*.

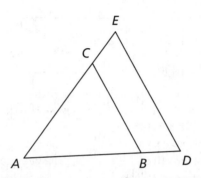

P **proportion** An equation stating that two ratios are equal.

proporción Una ecuación que enuncia que dos razones son iguales.

R **ratio** A ratio is a comparison of two quantities. It is sometimes expressed as a fraction. For example, suppose the length AB is 2 inches and the length *CD* is 3 inches. The ratio of the length of side *AB* to the length of side *CD* is 2 to 3, or $\frac{2}{3}$. The ratio of the length of side *CD* to the length of side *AB* is 3 to 2, or $\frac{3}{2}$.

razón La razón es una comparación de dos cantidades. A veces se expresa como una fracción. Por ejemplo, supón que la longitud de *AB* es 2 pulgadas y la longitud de *CD* es 3 pulgadas. La razón de la longitud del lado *AB* a la longitud del lado *CD* es de 2 a 3, es decir, $\frac{2}{3}$. La razón de la longitud del lado CD a la longitud del lado *AB* es 3 a 2, es decir, $\frac{3}{2}$.

relate Academic Vocabulary To have a connection or impact on something else.

related terms *connect, correlate*

sample: Find the area of the similar triangles below. Relate the area of triangle A to the area of triangle B.

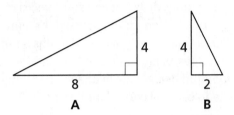

The area of triangle A is $\frac{1}{2}(4)(8) = 16$. The area of triangle B is $\frac{1}{2}(2)(4) = 4$. The area of triangle A is 4 times the area of triangle B.

relacionar Vocabulario académico Tener una conexión o un impacto en algo.

términos relacionados *conectar, correlacionar*

ejemplo: Halla el área de los triángulos semejantes de abajo. Relaciona el área del triángulo A con el área del triángulo B.

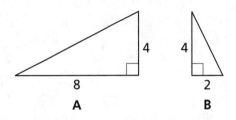

El área del triángulo A es $\frac{1}{2}(4)(8) = 16$. El área del triángulo B es $\frac{1}{2}(2)(4) = 4$. El área del triángulo A es 4 veces el área del triángulo B.

rep-tile A figure you can use to make a larger, similar version of the original is called a rep-tile. The smaller figure below is a rep-tile because you can use four copies of it to make a larger similar figure.

baldosa autosimilar Una figura que puedes usar para hacer una version más grande y semejante a la original, se llama baldosa autosimilar. La figura más pequeña de abajo es una baldosa autosimilar porque se pueden usar cuatro copias de ella para hacer una figura semejante más grande.

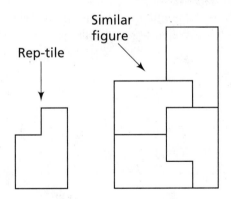

English/Spanish Glossary

S **scale drawing** An image of a figure that is similar to the original.

dibujo a escala La imagen de una figura que es semejante a la figura original.

scale factor The number used to multiply the lengths of a figure to stretch or shrink it to a similar image. If we use a scale factor of 3, all lengths in the image are 3 times as long as the corresponding lengths in the original. When you are given two similar figures, the scale factor is the ratio of the image side length to the corresponding original side length.

factor de escala El número utilizado para multiplicar las longitudes de una figura para ampliarla o reducirla a una imagen semejante. Si el factor de escala es 3, todas las longitudes de la imagen son 3 veces más largas que las longitudes correspondientes de la figura original. Cuando se dan dos figuras semejantes, el factor de escala es la razón de la longitud del lado de la imagen a la longitud del lado original correspondiente.

similar Similar figures have corresponding angles of equal measure and the ratios of each pair of corresponding sides are equivalent.

semejante Las figuras semejantes tienen ángulos correspondientes de igual medida y las razones de cada par de lados correspondientes son equivalentes.

Index

Index

Acknowledgments

Cover Design

Three Communication Design, Chicago

Photographs

Photo locators denoted as follows: Top (T), Center (C), Bottom (B), Left (L), Right (R), Background (Bkgd)

003 Mirek Weichsel/Glow Images; **007** Martin Heitner/Purestock/SuperStock; **010** Pearson Education, Inc.; **021** Bob Daemmrich/Alamy; **025** Tetra Images/ Alamy; **027** Pearson Education, Inc.; **033** Nikreates/Alamy; **053** AFP/Getty Images/Newscom; **080** Pearson Education, Inc.; **081** Pearson Education, Inc.; **083** Nikreates/Alamy; **089** Christian Carollo/Shutterstock; **093** Gary Blakeley/ Fotolia; **100** Izzet Keribar/Lonely planet Images/Getty Images; **102** Kevin Radford/Superstock; **109** Ableimages/Digital Vision/Thinkstock.